D0148396

GENDER *and* GENRE

THE UNIVERSITY OF NEW MEXICO PRESS • ALBUQUERQUE

GENDER *and* GENRE

An Introduction
to Women Writers
of Formula Westerns,
1900–1950

NORRIS YATES

Library of Congress Cataloging-in-Publication Data

Yates, Norris Wilson.
Gender and genre : an introduction to women writers
of formula westerns, 1900–1950 / Norris Yates.
p.   cm.
Includes bibliographical references and index.
ISBN 0-8263-1569-0 (cl)
1. Western stories—Women authors—History and
criticism. 2. Women and literature—West (U.S.)—
History—20th century, 3. American fiction—Women
authors—History and criticism. 4. American fiction—
20th century—History and criticism. 5. American
fiction—West (U.S.)—History and criticism. 6. West
(U.S.)—In literature.   I. Title.
PS374.W4Y38   1995
813'.0874099287—dc20   94-32020

Designed by Miss Linda Mae Tratechaud

for
KAREN AND MARK

ACKNOWLEDGMENTS

The making of this monograph was expedited by research grants from Iowa State University, Ames, Iowa, and by the cooperation of efficient and friendly staff at the Parks Library, Iowa State University; the Knight Library, University of Oregon; and the library of Oklahoma State University. Additional help came from Professor Christine Bold of the University of Guelph, Guelph, Ontario, who offered useful suggestions about the substance of this book; from Margaret E. Shaw of Grants Pass, Oregon, who procured data on Vingie E. Roe's residence in that state; and from W. Ross Yates and Catherine Gleason Yates, of McMinnville, Oregon, who copyread the typescript and saved me from several lapses of logic and numerous lapses of style. My thanks to all. Larry Borosky improved this work through a superb job of copy editing. I alone of course am responsible for any deficiencies in this book.

Thanks also to the Boise State University Press for permission to use herein portions of my booklet *Carolyn Lockhart* (Western Writers Series #116).

Norris W. Yates
Eugene, Oregon

CONTENTS

INTRODUCTION

Lillian S. Robinson has written that feminist literary study has included "the discovery, republication, and reappraisal of 'lost' or undervalued writers and their work. . . . [R]eputations have been reborn or remade and a female countercanon has come into being, out of components that were largely unavailable even a dozen years ago."[1] My original intent with the present book was simply to carry this trend into study of the formula Western. However, the venture evolved into an introduction to the work of several women writers in this genre who attracted some attention in their time but since have been largely neglected. As research progressed, I developed several other purposes. One was to show that even though these women seem to have worked independently of each other, their fiction as a body constitutes a definite subgenre within the genre of the formula Western. Jane Tompkins has stated that "when women wrote about the West, the stories they told did not look anything like what we know as the Western."[2] She was partly right. The women I discuss wrote formula Westerns, but formula Westerns with a difference.

Another purpose was to explore the possibility that, rather than having been adapted from the dime novel, as Henry Nash Smith and other scholars have assumed, heroines in Western fiction, especially in Western fiction by women, tended to resemble heroines in the domestic novel.[3] This exploration has led to the discovery of the reincarnation, or resurrection, of one type of domestic heroine thought to have died out. Referring to many nineteenth-century novels by women, Nina Baym has said that they tell "a single tale . . . the story of a young girl who is deprived of the supports she had rightly or wrongly depended on to sustain her throughout life and is faced with the necessity of winning her own way in the world."[4] Baym's comment fits most of the heroines discussed or cited in the present work. However, the prevailing heroine type in Westerns by women (appearing also in some Westerns by men) is not the dainty, ornamental image of "True Womanhood" promoted in a number of nineteenth-century domestic novels but a contrasting image, termed by Frances B. Cogan the "Ideal of Real Womanhood." This image circulated even more prominently than the True Woman image but was paid little attention by historians of culture until publication of Cogan's study, *All-American Girl* (1989). Drawing on "advice" books and articles as well as on domestic fiction, Cogan found that the image of the Ideal Real Woman included physical fitness, formal education (up to and sometimes including college), and the ability to earn a living outside the home if necessary. In courtship the Ideal Real Woman showed clearheadedness and rationality rather than romantic infatuation, and she had the right to independently choose a marriage partner, and after marriage, to enjoy his companionship rather than to endure his domination.

A woman's sphere was still the home, but if mistreated she could leave, taking the children with her, though divorce was taboo. Further, the image was associated with the possibility of gainful employment after as well as before marriage.

Cogan says that "the Ideal of Real Womanhood vanished as an identifiable entity sometime after 1880 and has never been seen again, except in fragments."[5] However, most heroines of woman-authored Westerns were reincarnations of the Ideal Real Woman— with two modifications. Both are attributable in part to the Western's incorporation of the romance plot, a standard component of travel and adventure fiction as well as of most domestic tales. Among other qualities the romance plot, as Rachel Blau DuPlessis has said, "values sexual asymmetry, including the division of labor by gender, is based on extremes of sexual difference, and evokes an aura around the couple itself. In short, the romance plot, broadly speaking, is a trope for the sex-gender system as a whole."[6] The Western formula requirement of a fast pace and plenty of physical action made it convenient for authors to speed up the romance plot and to evoke the "aura" by making one or both of the romantic leads fall in love quickly and intensely if sometimes unconsciously. The initial modification, therefore, was a tendency for the heroine to fall in love at first sight whether the hero did or not (often he also did; sometimes he fell first).

The second modification was that the heroine frequently functioned as an agent for rehabilitating flawed males, a function that Cogan finds, on the whole, discouraged in the domestic novel.[7] However, in the Western women were a civilizing force, and helping potential heroes free themselves from cowardice, bad temper, alcoholism, and moral confusion was part of the civilizing process.

One should add that a substantial minority of heroines in women's Westerns did qualify fully as Ideal Real Women—i.e., without the two differences. Rosemary Allen in B. M. Bower's *The Flying U's Last Stand*, Susie MacDonald in Caroline Lockhart's *"Me— Smith,"* and Belle Dawson in Vingie E. Roe's *Black Belle Rides the Uplands* are among those heroines who neither fall in love at first sight nor try to rehabilitate struggling males. With or without the two modifications designated, the Ideal Real Woman in Westerns offered a contrast to the New Woman of the Progressive Era and to the flapper of the 1910s and 1920s. She was also a manifestation of nostalgia. Perpetrators of the Western invoked values associated with the rural past, including a lost frontier, and looked backward in time to the female image that had pervaded the domestic novel for an earlier readership.

A third purpose of this book is to apply certain concepts developed by Elaine Showalter, Sandra M. Gilbert, and Susan Gubar to the analysis of these rediscovered formula Westerns by women. Showalter says nineteenth-century women's writing was a "coded response to male images, influences, and texts, a form of protest against patriarchal literary authority."[8] In women's fiction, this protest often took the form of a "double-voiced discourse, containing a 'dominant' and a 'muted' story, what Gilbert and Gubar call a 'palimpsest,' in the reading of which "one must keep two alternative oscillating tests simultaneously in view."[9] In "palimpsestic" writing, "the surface designs conceal or obscure deeper, less accessible (and less socially acceptable) levels of meaning. Thus these authors managed the difficult task of achieving true female literary authority by simultaneously conforming to and subverting patriarchal literary standards."[10]

Use of the palimpsestic strategy by women writers of formula Westerns is herein shown to have been extensive. Examination of this strategy helps to answer a question made more pressing by Jane Tompkins' view that, in its secular morality, antifeminist bent, and repression of feeling, the Western responded negatively to the Christian morality, female dominance, and emotionalism of the domestic novel with "a reaction that looks very much like literary gender war."[11] By writing from within the male camp in this "gender war" and using the double-voiced strategy, intentionally or otherwise, women authors could bore from within, still get published, and to some degree resolve the conflict between the demands of the macho Western and their feminist leanings. Another result of this strategy was formal kinship with the major women writers cited by Showalter, Gilbert, and Gubar as having used it. However different were the goals and achievements of a Charlotte Brontë or a Doris Lessing from those of American women who wrote Westerns for mass consumption, a strategic tie binding all of them together originated in similarity of gender and of the inferior status prescribed for that gender by the male-oriented literary and publishing establishment.

A frequent method of conveying an indirect message was the creation of women protagonists, which occurred much more often in Westerns by women than by men. Saul David has commented that "the woman in the Western has always played an inconsequential role—subtract the rancher's daughter or the dance hall queen from the run of the mill western story and nothing in the story line is changed."[12] Though probably valid for Westerns by men, this generalization is not valid for those by women. Female protagonists in novels by men do come to mind, such as Zane Grey's Jane Withersteen and Joan Randle (in *Riders of the Purple Sage* and *The Border Legion*, respectively), but they were exceptional, whereas in Westerns by women, aside from those by B. M. Bower, female leads were the rule rather than the exception. In and of itself, presenting a woman as the main character implied that a woman could be more interesting and more important than presumed by the conventions of the genre. Moreover, whenever a Western heroine—that is, the resurrected Western version of the Ideal Real Woman—had to make her own way, she did so ably and thereby broadcast a message, however low the volume, that in adversity a woman could do almost anything a man could do—and maybe could do it just as well even without the adversity.

One way in which women authors muted the messages about competence and self-reliance conveyed through active heroines was by propelling these heroines into domesticity at closure. The romance plot required a "happy" ending that included marriage and homemaking for the female lead. Nonetheless, every one of the women authors discussed herein attempted in some of her novels to stretch, bend, twist, or otherwise alter and manipulate the traditional ending, toward allowing the heroine to retain a portion of her premarital individuality and independence without offending any literary or social convention. Such alterations were among the significant ways in which these authors supported and yet subverted Western-style images of ideal femininity and male hegemony.

Two further, interrelated differences of Westerns by women from those by men may here be identified briefly. First, novels by women included relatively less violence, in particular, less gunplay. Second, Westerns by women also included greater frequency of indoor settings, especially homes.

꿈

Readers who might otherwise expect too much from this rather specialized monograph are hereby warned that the selection of certain works for analysis in detail has meant rejection of other works for one reason or another, sometimes because they could not be considered examples of the formula Western. Rejects include novels of frontier farm settlement, such as Sheba Hargreaves's *The Cabin at the Trail's End* (1928) and Bess Streeter Aldrich's *A Lantern in Her Hand* (1928), and fiction by authors who specialized in critical and realistic explorations of a particular state or region, e.g., Gertrude

Atherton and Geraldine Bonner, re-creators of the California past, and the Edna Ferber of *Cimarron* and *Giant.* Excluded also are "wagons west" fictions, although one of "my" authors, Vingie E. Roe, composed several such. Finally, an indefinite number of women writers in the genre have not been mentioned because they have not been rediscovered, at least by the present researcher. This book is merely an introduction to a subgenre some of whose creators are still "out there."

Another disclaimer concerns definition of the formula Western. The definition used in this book is based on material drawn mostly from the "slicks" (magazines printed on glossy paper with a high rag content), rather than from the "pulps" (periodicals printed on cheaper paper derived mostly from pulpwood), for two reasons. One is the impossibility of separating writers of pulp Westerns by gender because of the frequent use of pseudonyms by pulp authors, especially by those most prolific (Frederick Faust used at least twenty pseudonyms in marketing 196 novels and many shorter pieces).[13] Daisy Bacon, a sometime pulp editor for the Street & Smith Company, informed one scholar that although the firm's "romance westerns" had an almost entirely female readership, "55% of these stories were written by men."[14] She did not say how many Street & Smith authors of both genders may have used pseudonyms or names ambiguous as to gender such as B. M. Bower (a pseudonym) and Eli Colter (a real name). Both authors were women.

The second reason is that Westerns ascribable with certainty to women did indeed appear more often in the slicks. Of the authors introduced in this book, only B. M. Bower and Cherry Wilson published extensively in the pulps, although most of their longer fiction eventually became available in hard binding.

As a geographical term, what does "Western" in the phrase "formula Western" mean? For purposes of this book, spatially the West is the area west of the Missouri, south of the tundra, and north of the Sierra Madre. Temporally this West existed from the end of the Civil War until about the end of the 1920s. As for action, one prolific author of Westerns, Frank Gruber, once reduced all plots to seven basic, fast-paced narrative types, admittedly with some overlap.[15] In summary form, these are:

The "epic" of construction (often of a railroad or dam).
The ranch story (often ranchers against rustlers).
The empire story, often like the ranch story, but "on the
    grand scale. . . . The conflict is between titans of the West"
    (185).
The avenger tale (about righting a wrong on behalf of a
    person or persons other than the hero; sometimes the
    heroine is the character benefited).
Custer's last stand (variations on the theme of cavalry versus
    Indians).
The outlaw story.
The Marshal story.

Along with a Western setting and one of these standardized plots, three other qualities mark the mainstream Western. One is the simple clash of good with evil. Another is an attitude toward the Old West that may be summarized thus: The West brought out the best and worst in people; it rewarded the good with adventure, romance, and usually prosperity; it punished the bad, usually with violent death. The third quality was simply the male chauvinism of adventure fiction in general carried to an extreme.

In this book, then, the term "formula Western" denotes fiction appearing primarily in the slicks, set in the space and time described above, and featuring lots of action, a simplistic morality, a West that developed character (though character was usually subordinated to action), and consistent machismo. Often in the pulps, and nearly always in the slicks, the formula also incorporated the traditional romance plot of much other popular fiction.

THE FORMULA WESTERN AND HOW IT GREW

"It is not likely," warns John R. Milton, "that any one writer invented the complete [Western] formula or suggested variations which might be played on it." Milton joins John G. Cawelti in giving some credit for the rise of the formula Western to James Fenimore Cooper, Bret Harte, and Edward Ellis of dime novel fame.[1] Precursors of the formula named by other commentators include Ann Sophia Stephens, E.Z.C. Judson (Ned Buntline), and Edward Wheeler.[2] According to Henry Nash Smith in *Virgin Land,* dime novels "lead almost in a straight line from the Beadle publications to the Westerns of the present day"—in his case, 1949.[3] Smith's comments on the dime novel heroine hold special interest. He says some dime novelists escaped a gentility that included female passivity by transforming the heroine into a Native American girl who later proved to be a white long ago captured by tribespeople.[4] In the twentieth-century Western, this female often became a ranch girl who could ride and shoot but had been to boarding school or college in the East. As for the ungenteel tomboys and Amazons in the dime novel—the Calamity Janes, Hurricane Nells, and Klondike Kits, along with genuine Native American girls—they often were killed saving the hero's life or helping him in some other way. Those that lived sometimes remained friends with the hero, but the really uncouth types rarely turned into romantic heroines headed for domesticity. In the formula Western, these less-than-respectable but not evil types reappeared in various guises in works by both men and women.

Examples include Judy Norcross, tomboyish daughter of the villain in Jackson Gregory's *Redwood and Gold,* and Rose Ivory, a saloon singer and hero's helper in Vingie E. Roe's *Black Belle Rides the Uplands.*

However, the domestic novel exercised a significant influence on women writers of formula Westerns. It probably influenced a number of male writers of Westerns, too, although this supposition awaits further study. The following comments on the influence of the domestic novel on the Western should therefore be taken as applying only to works in the Western genre by women.

To begin with, novels both domestic and Western usually included a romantic plot leading to marriage and a prospective "career" for the heroine as wife and homemaker. Second, novels in both categories included heroines who were social outcasts, alone in the world, often because their mother, father, or both were dead, missing, physically handicapped, or mentally unstable. In both genres the absence or inadequacy of fathers seems more important than that of mothers. Frances B. Cogan finds the weak father or father surrogate (often a teacher or informal counselor) a frequent problem for domestic heroines from 1850–1870.[6] A third similarity of domestic and Western novels is the Jane-Rochester relationship, what Helen Waite Papashvily has called "the mutilation of the male."[7] The hero is brought low by gunshot, accident, exposure, or illness; the heroine can dominate him temporarily as a nurse and mother figure, and the hero, as Elaine Showalter points out, finds what it's like to be helpless and dominated—that is, in a female situation. One message of the domestic and Western novels in which such disabling of the hero occurs is: "If he is . . . to rediscover his humanity, the 'woman's man' must find out how it feels to be a woman."[8] It should not be forgotten, however, that in many fictional contexts a woman nursing a man is essentially a servant, though perhaps a special kind of servant.

To imply with no further comment that the formula Western developed from the domestic novel and the dime novel would be to overlook the fairly complex details of how the Western formula actually grew and how that growth was nurtured directly by women authors. The nature and status of the Western heroine during the early growth period of the formula needs special consideration.

Owen Wister's *The Virginian* (1902) has been much discussed, but no one has emphasized that Wister credited a woman with a part of his inspiration: "It was a happy day" when he read "the first sagebrush story by Mary Hallock Foote."[9] What fiction by Ms. Foote he may have had in mind is not clear, but her earliest novel, *The Led-Horse Claim* (1883), was set in a Colorado mining camp based on an area wherein the author had resided with her husband, a mining engineer. The protagonist is a young woman from the East who cannot accept violence even in defense of right. When the hero kills her weak, villainous brother, she rejects his love, and the romance moves toward marriage only after she has nursed him through a serious illness, during which he becomes a "woman's man" and understands her feelings more clearly than before. In this novel, a "modest best seller,"[10] two other, interrelated themes also appeared that later became part of the budding Western formula: the education, after a fashion, of an Eastern woman by the West, and the necessity at times for righteous violence to combat unrighteous violence.

With some justice, *The Led-Horse Claim* could be labeled the first formula Western, and much of Foote's later fiction also included themes, characters, and action sequences that eventually became staple ingredients of the formula-Western genre. The romance plot was one such sequence. However, in Foote's narratives the romance plot is sometimes undermined by a skepticism about marriage conveyed in the low-key manner defined by Elaine Showalter and her colleagues. For example, the title of one short story that ends happily— that is, with prospective marriage—is "The Maid's Progress." The analogy of this title to William Hogarth's rake, whose progress is from bad to worse, insinuates doubt about this maid's future happiness as a matron. Moreover, the author-narrator at one point remarks, "The founding of a family is essentially an egotistic and ungenerous proceeding."[11] The ending in marriage carries the dominant, socially approved message of the story; the narrator's comment conveys a different and less socially acceptable communication—muted because it can be considered negated by the ending, as can the skepticism implied in the title.

Wister backed more or less unintentionally into the mind-set that helped produce *The Virginian.* He tried to make the first part of *Lin McLean* (1897) realistic, especially in depicting Katie Peck, who seduces Lin into marriage. Lin is twenty-four years old and good-hearted but far from heroic. Katie, a biscuit-shooter (waitress), is ten years older but passes—with Lin—for twenty-seven. In the patronizing language of the Eastern narrator, "she was handsome in a large California-fruit style. They made a good-looking pair of animals."[12] After Katie has died from drug addiction, Lin participates in a thoroughly conventional romance plot with an idealized, stereotyped heroine.

In *The Virginian,* Wister depicts the West as it should have been rather than as it was. A large readership has enjoyed this Western romance between a cowpuncher whose geographic background suggests aristocracy and good manners and a young New England woman of genteel, upper-middle-class provenance. The Virginian was one of the first cowboy characters to personalize the conflict between order and the violence needed to establish that order in the fictional West. As Russel B. Nye points out, through *The Virginian,* Wister also fixed "the walkdown firmly in western tradition, that is, the climax in which two gunmen approach each other on an empty street until one draws."[13] In addition, as John L. Cobbs says, Wister pulled together other aspects of the cowboy figure—the iconography—horse, gun, clothing—and the behavior patterns—"the intense, almost athletic physical activism; the spontaneity; the stoicism and understated acceptance of hardship; . . . the chivalric ritualization of 'code' behavior whether in treatment of men or women, the profound self-respect."[14]

Of Molly Stark Wood, the heroine, the author admitted that his characterization was "a failure. She seems to me without personality."[15] Small wonder that she seemed thus. Into a romance of Western adventure Wister had brought, with virtually no change, a stereotype from the domestic novel: the Ideal Real Woman. Like dozens of her predecessors, Molly earns her own living, shows coolness and skill as a nurse, and critically evaluates her suitor's manners and personality. Other male writers of Westerns in the early twentieth century tended to individualize their heroines even less than did Wister. Emerson Hough, who in *North of 36* depicted cowboys realistically and a superfluous heroine unrealistically, declared that "the chief figure of the American West was . . . the gaunt, sad-faced woman sitting on the front seat of the wagon."[16] Why then did Hough not depict such women effectively in his fiction? Surely because, although as commentator he was writing about the real, historical West, as novelist he had accepted a formula that included an idealized female image suitable for casting in the standard romance plot.

Elizabeth Ammons has shown that the turn of the century and the two decades that followed it saw a surge of creative writing by women who aspired to artistic excellence and sometimes achieved that goal. She examines fiction by seventeen women writers, of whom Edith Wharton, Willa Cather, Ellen Glasgow, and Gertrude Stein are today the best known, and also discusses six black women authors, one Chinese American, and one Native American.[17] Her subjects lie outside the scope of the present study, but it should be noted that while this wave of feminine creativity was rising in the realm of high art, something parallel was going on at the lower level of mass-market Westerns. Before *The Virginian* and at about the time Wister's landmark novel appeared, several women wrote novels about the West that included elements of the as yet uncrystallized formula as well as elements that deviated from the formula. In *Squaw Élouise* (1892), Marah Ellis Ryan presents a Native American heroine who, conventionally, dies and thereby sets the hero free to marry a white woman—but not until the heroine has moved the plot actively and therefore unconventionally. In *With Hoops of Steel* (1900), Florence Finch Kelly offers a version of the ranch story (number two in Frank Gruber's list of formula plots) but also devotes considerable space to a second-lead Latina heroine who dominates one long sequence in the narrative.[18]

In 1902, the year of *The Virginian*, Frances McElrath's *The Rustler: A Tale of Love and War in Wyoming* appeared. Here was another ranch story, but interwoven was a romance plot differing widely from the usual secular, marriage-oriented blueprint. Near the end the hero is fatally shot, but before he dies, the heroine teaches him about God and about how "His great plan is to make every one of us learn through suffering" (415–416). The heroine has been engaged to a man she does not love; after the hero's death she renounces her fiancé, literally gives him to another woman, and plans to devote the rest of her life to helping the children of former rustlers.

Gwendolen Overton followed *The Heritage of Unrest* (1901), a nonformulaic novel about a half-blood Apache woman, with *The Golden Chain* (1903), in which a reformed prostitute-with-heart-of-gold moves the plot crucially and unconventionally by rescuing the equally stereotyped ingénue of a heroine from a crowd offended by her performance in a traveling show. In this novel the hero does little, which in itself constitutes a departure from the developing Western formula. In Frances Parker's *Marjie of the Lower Ranch* (1903), the heroine marries rashly but loses her villainous husband to fatal violence before consummation; she remains conventionally virginal for the hero at the end (in that respect she anticipates by nine years Caroline Lockhart's rashly married and quickly widowed Essie Tisdale in *The Lady Doc*). Parker's *Hope Hathaway* (1904) is also a formula ranch story—except that the schoolteacher heroine, instead of functioning mainly as passive victim and informant, rescues the hero from the rustlers and dominates the tale throughout.[19]

One male author who during the early years of the formula Western paid more than token attention to women in his Western fiction was Alfred Henry Lewis. His reputation as a writer of Westerns depends mainly on *Wolfville* (1897) and other collections of Wolfville stories.[20] The last, *Faro Nell and Her Friends*, appeared in 1913, the year after Zane Grey's landmark *Riders of the Purple Sage*. Most of the pieces in the Wolfville collections are reminiscences about an Arizona mining town rendered in dialect by an "Old Cattleman." On the whole, the Wolfville males are a set of comic roughnecks, but the few women residents of this town are not only civilizers but members of a female subcommunity that may not have a counterpart anywhere in early Western fiction. Mrs. Rucker, the "middle-aged" (she's twenty-eight) manager of the hotel and restaurant, is married to a male hero who deserts her but is brought back forcibly by the wife's well-meaning male friends. Benson Annie at first works for Mrs. Rucker but soon opens her own business, a laundry, and shortly thereafter gets married. Tucson Jennie, briefly another employee of Mrs. Rucker, becomes a wife and in due time a mother. Marriage puts all of these women into homemaking but not into oblivion; with Faro Nell, a gambler's fancy woman, these wives function as a domestic sisterhood, all four women actively supporting one another.

At the "Red Light" saloon, gambler Cherokee Hall runs a faro bank, and Faro Nell, his lookout, sits by his side. Nell is unique in two respects. First, as just noted, she interacts on an equal basis with the "respectable" women of the community. For example, she joins Mrs. Rucker, Mrs. Tutt (the former Tucson Jennie), and several of the men in opposing the views of a typed suffragette agitator, Cynthiana Bark, who has invaded Wolfville from the East.[21] Second, though lacking benefit of clergy, the relationship of Nell and Cherokee parallels that of a harmoniously married small-business couple whose attitudes are somewhat—but for the times and the genre, not excessively—patriarchal. Cherokee shares his winnings with Nell, and when Doc Holliday cleans out Cherokee at the faro game, Nell wins all the money back and insists on dividing it equally between them—"Don't you-all tell me we're partners?"[22] The women of Wolfville do not systematically question the dominance of men, but Lewis's female characters show more variety in their behavior and move plots more often and more significantly than do women in most Westerns written by men a few years later.

Lewis had shown a twofold interest in women as domestic servants of males, and inconsistently, as self-reliant builders of their own lives. Zane Grey, one of the few writers before 1920 who still has some works in print, shared this inconsistency. With *Riders of the Purple Sage* (1912), Grey became the first male writer of longer Western fiction to make a woman the protagonist. In subsequent works Grey presented other female protagonists; even so, Richard Etulain may be right in calling *Riders* "Grey's most famous but perhaps least typical novel."[23] However, Teresa Jordan notes ironically that the strength of Jane Withersteen, the heroine, is "passive—as a woman's should be."[24] At the end, Jane and Lassiter the hero, seclude themselves with a foster child in a natural hideaway. Although their relationship is illicit, Jane goes into a future as a mother and homemaker; no matter that the "home" is as big as Surprise Valley, if not as all outdoors. Yet *Riders* stands as an example of the formula when it was still relatively flexible and had not been hardened by dozens of replications. A few male authors besides Grey produced variations on the heroine image, but none that I know of who wrote before the 1950s made significant alterations in the Western maid's progress from self-reliance and virginity to dependence within the marital state.[25]

The foregoing sketch of the formula Western's development suggests that certain ingredients of the domestic novel, most prominently the romance plot and the Ideal Real Woman as protagonist, were to some degree absorbed by male as well as female authors of Westerns. Mary Hallock Foote and Owen Wister blended realism with idealizing and stereotyping. Around the turn of the century, several women wrote Westerns in which active heroines dominated the narratives. Alfred Henry Lewis offered variety in his women characters to an extent uncommon among male authors at that time and for about fifty years thereafter. Zane Grey, a major developer of the formula, also became one of its most frequent manipulators, but few of his later contemporaries significantly liberalized their heroines' functions and fates.[26]

However, like their female predecessors, several women who built careers as writers of formula Westerns during the early twentieth century cautiously but definitely loosened the chains that bound formula heroines. How these authors did so is examined in the following chapters.

2

B. M. BOWER AND
THE HAPPY FAMILY

Peaceful it was, and home-like and contentedly prosperous; a little world tucked away in its hills, with its own little triumphs and defeats, its own heartaches and rejoicings; a lucky little world.[1]

In 1926, Douglas Branch asserted that "the most cuddled, the most admired, of all the cowboy heroes has been Chip of the Flying U."[2] Chip was the creation of the prolific B. M. Bower, whose 68 books and more than 150 novelettes and short stories may have had more than 2 million readers. Although this figure shrinks when compared with the 40 million estimated at one time for Zane Grey's books and the 190 million for those of Louis L'Amour,[3] Bower's fiction clearly did attain some popularity.

Orrin Engen has written a brief biography of Bower and added an indispensable bibliography of her writings. A few other students of Western fiction have also written about her and her work.[4] Yet much remains unsaid about Bower's narratives, and no one has commented on her contribution to the domestic element in the formula Western.

"Ladies may read this story, so I am not going to pretend to repeat the things they [a bunch of angry cowboys] said." In this passage from *Flying U Ranch* (167), as well as in many other authorial comments, Bower induced at least some of her readers to believe that she was a man. She also encouraged this misapprehension by sometimes telling the main story from a first-person, male viewpoint—for example, in *The Range Dwellers* and *The Dry Ridge Gang.* Her frequent depictions of stereotyped heroes and heroines did nothing to dispel the illusion, which persisted even after death in 1940 had ended her long career.[5] However, with hindsight one may now see in Bower's work a woman coping with the restrictions of the formula Western and, in so doing, helping to create a special kind of fiction. Within the subgenre of the woman-authored formula Western, Bower and a few other women developed what may be called a sub-subgenre, the domestic Western novel.

Examining books by American women in the eighteenth and nineteenth centuries, feminist scholar Annette Kolodny found projected in the "domestic novel of western relocation"—that is, of frontier farm settlement—a New World landscape that was "not merely an object of dominance and exploitation" but "a maternal 'garden,' receiving and nurturing human children."[6] Although Bower wrote more about men than about women and children, her Happy Family novels were essentially domestic novels of ranch life. In them the "garden" is the cattle ranch and is paternal rather than maternal. Her cowboy heroes participate in a quasi-family lifestyle, of which the physical and psychological center—the home—is the ranch bunkhouse. Such homemaking as occurs is accomplished largely by the "boys" themselves (even meals are prepared by a male cook). Chip's wife Della, who appears in the first Happy Family novel as an unmarried physician, is thereafter influential from time to time, but the presiding parental figure is ranch co-owner J. G. Whitmore, the "Old Man." However, despite making him a lifelong bachelor, the author surely had no antifeminist intent in creating the "homelike" little world of the Flying U. Writing of the movie *Three Men and a Baby* and other films in which groups of males take over child care, Tania Modleski states that such productions reveal "men's desire to usurp women's procreative function."[7] However, I have not found indications of this sort in Happy Family fiction, or for that matter in any Western that is in part about surrogate parenthood. On the contrary, in all of these pieces a profeminist proposition is implied—namely, that insofar as men do child care, women gain freedom from the maternal burden.

Della's influence becomes significant whenever she practices her profession on personnel from the bunkhouse, and it usually includes helping her patients to better understand the position of women. Having been treated and nursed by "the Little Doctor" after an injury, Chip himself is the first Happy Family member to become what Elaine Showalter has called a "woman's man," a male who through weakness or desirability has found out "how it feels to be a woman."[8] In addition to employing this strategy of bringing down (or bringing up?) the males, Bower also speaks frequently with the double voice, simultaneously presenting an overt, conventional message and a muted communication that is "less socially acceptable."[9] The latter message is often critical of the patriarchal values promoted by Wister and other male writers of Westerns.

❧

B. M. Bower was born Bertha Muzzy in Minnesota in 1871. When she was nineteen, her parents moved to a ranch in Choteau County, northern Montana.[10] Bower's fiction suggests that she reacted sympathetically and creatively to ranch life and the rugged landscape and perhaps also to her labor as a schoolteacher "boarding round." She got considerable experience as an instructor, even though in that pioneer country her own schooling had consisted of "sporadic private tutoring."[11] In 1890 she married Clayton J. Bower. Engen says that the "nineteen-year-old girl married him to spite her family, and that this marriage was not a happy one for her."[12] The marriage did last eleven years and produced a daughter and two sons. By 1905, after Bertha had begun publishing fiction, she had also divorced Bower (although she kept his name for authorial purposes) and married William Bertram Sinclair, a cousin of Upton Sinclair and himself eventually author of eleven formula Westerns. The Sinclairs had one daughter but separated in 1911. Ten years later, at fifty, Bertha married an old friend, a former top cowhand, bronc buster, and county sheriff named William (Bud) Cowan, for whose book of reminiscences, *Range Rider,* she wrote an introduction.

Chip of the Flying U, her first novel, appeared in 1906. On the

Flying U ranch, the Happy Family consists of the household residents and the bunkhouse gang. About this circle Bower wrote fifteen books; taken as a body, these constitute Bower's most original contribution to the Western. In the early scenes of *Chip*, the ranch house branch of this extended family includes only Whitmore, his sister Della, and Louise Bixby (the Countess), a talkative divorcee who functions as housekeeper and house cook. Bunkhouse-based employees include a cook and single cowboys ranging from five to fifteen in number depending on the job needs of the ranch during any given season. In 1924 Bower referred to one of her early novels, *The Lure of the Dim Trails* (1907), as having been set "in 1886 or thereabouts."[13] The Happy Family beginnings are also set at about that time—when the open-range cattle business had just passed its peak and begun its permanent decline. The fictional time in the Flying U series spans about twenty years and ends with the events in *Rodeo* (1928). In that novel, the Old West has gone, and the only way the now-grown son of Chip and Della can be a "re'l ol' cow-puncher, still"[14] is to ride the rodeo circuit. His first appearance in big-time rodeo is the occasion for a reunion of the Happy Family. Most of them have been long gone from the home ranch, yet most are still single: "They intended to marry and settle down—sometime. But there was always something in the way of carrying those intentions to fulfillment, so that eventually the majority of the Happy Family found themselves . . . drifting along toward permanent bachelorhood." What was that something? Clearly, they preferred the "freedom of the bunk-house"[15]—that is, modified domesticity through a largely male bonding—over full domesticity as husbands and fathers. Yet none of them rode into the distance like Shane or the Lone Ranger.

The Happy Family books are here listed in order of publication, which, like that of Cooper's Leatherstocking novels, differs from the order of events depicted therein. For example, *The Whoop-Up Trail* and three subsequent novels feature the adventures of Chip before he meets Della. Further, as noted, the fictional time span of the Happy Family fiction is about twenty years, whereas the time span between publication of the first Chip story (1904)[16] and *The*

Family Failing (published posthumously) is thirty-seven years. The list:

> *Chip of the Flying U* (1906). Novel.
> *The Lonesome Trail* (1909). Short stories.
> *The Happy Family* (1910). Short stories.
> *Flying U Ranch* (1912). Novel.
> *The Flying U's Last Stand* (1915). Novel.
> *Jean of the Lazy A* (1915). Novel. (No Happy Family characters appear, but Jean and several other characters from this work appear subsequently in *The Phantom Herd* and *The Heritage of the Sioux* along with members of the Happy Family.)
> *The Phantom Herd* (1916). Novel.
> *The Heritage of the Sioux* (1916). Novel.
> *Rodeo* (1928). Novel.
> *Dark Horse: A Story of the Flying U* (1931). Novel.
> *The Whoop-Up Trail* (1933) Novel.
> *The Flying U Strikes* (1934). Novel.
> *Trouble Rides the Wind* (1935). Novel.
> *Man on Horseback* (1940). Novel.
> *The Spirit of the Range* (1940). Novel.
> *The Family Failing* (1941). Short stories.

In the Flying U ranch house, with the Countess as housekeeper, Dr. Della has a great deal of freedom to function as the only reliable physician in a rather large chunk of Montana. One may doubt that the Countess has exactly a life-fulfilling role; after *Chip* she is almost invisible except when others praise the cooking in which she takes pride and on a notable occasion when she and Della, at the moment more sisters than employer and employee, participate in the practical joke of curling the hair on a cowboy's fringed chaps.[17] As for the children one expects to find in a group designated as a family, we need only stretch the term "children" to include the single cowpunchers most of the time. Then, to a considerable degree the Flying U ranch is indeed a paternal garden "receiving and nurturing children." The six-gun mystique is conspicuous by its absence; instead of gunplay there is horseplay, including the kind of rough-and-tumble fighting teachers break up on playgrounds. The male Family members deal in mature fashion with the skills and hardships of ranch work, but in personal relationships with each other and with women they often show immaturity. They haze a new employee with schoolboy relentlessness; later, in repentance, they bear themselves "very much as do children who have quarrelled foolishly."[18] *The Family Failing* includes several short stories about the title topic, which is a tendency of the group to hector with immature humor any member who betrays an adult feeling—usually affection for a woman. It could be argued that this tendency is a defense against the breach of Happy Family unity by females, but during the first few years of the Flying U cycle three women—Della Whitmore, the Countess, and Rosemary Allen—are admitted to the Family circle.

Despite the title, Della is the real protagonist of *Chip of the Flying U*. In this novel, one theme prominent earlier in Wister's *The Virginian* and Frances McElrath's *The Rustler*—the initiation of an Eastern woman into Western ways—is varied by the initiation of this heroine into a masculine but quite domestic circle. Having completed medical training, Della, age twenty-three, comes to the Flying U for a vacation at the suggestion of its co-owner, an older brother. She is no orphaned and penniless waif, but in a practical sense she is alone with no strong attachments—she has not seen the brother for many years. Before she arrives, certain popular female stereotypes draw good-natured satire from the author. One type is the dainty True Woman as she might react out West. Chip Bennett (age twenty-four) wonders if she's one of "the Sweet Young Things, that faint away at sight of a six-shooter, and squawk and catch at your arm if they see a garter snake, and blush if you happen to catch their eye suddenly." He then worries that maybe she's "the other kind"—that is, the emancipated New Woman who will "wear double-barrelled skirts [bloomers] and . . . try to go the men one better in everything" (18–19, omissions mine). Nevertheless, love rapidly descends on Della and Chip and in Chip's case is reinforced when Della sets the broken leg of his favorite horse. "A broken bone is a broken bone," she tells Chip, "whether it belongs to a man—or some *other* beast" (58, original emphasis). On the surface, the heroine is comically putting down the man into whose arms she will eventually fall; the subtextual communication is that a serious comparison between human and animal males would not necessarily favor the human.

Aside from the immediacy of her interest in Chip, Della is one of those capable, self-possessed Ideal Real Women whose predecessors Frances B. Cogan found in the domestic novel. During a dance at the ranch, she copes effectively with an emergency: Seven small children have gotten into her stock of medicines. Having commandeered the assistance of Chip and Weary, another cowhand, she pumps the small stomachs. Though handling the "flying heels and squirming bodies" seems to the two men "very much like branding calves" (112), the usual roles of male and female are in a sense reversed. The Little Doctor (already known around the ranch by that nickname) is the person in charge; Chip and Weary are flunkies.

In the early part of this novel, the palimpsest method is also used in reverse. Instead of being muted, the socially questionable message about Della is the dominant one. Insofar as she can shoot a coyote, laugh off hazing, doctor a horse, and turn cowboys into pediatric orderlies, Dr. Della Whitmore resembles the nonconformist New Woman, but she also demonstrates that a woman who accomplishes certain traditionally male tasks may yet play the roles expected of the female. She has said that "it's just fun to keep house" (69), and the reader already knows that she and Chip have fallen in love. In addition, she has handled a domestic crisis involving small children; these facts implicitly reassure the reader that she not only qualifies for membership in the Happy Family but that she also will be properly domesticated as the hero's wife and the mother of his offspring.

As in most romance plots, several unfortunate incidents roughen the course of true love. Through these incidents the author sends out an undertone of comments on the oppression of women. For example, when Chip tries to break an ornery bronc, Della, piqued by his momentary aloofness, sympathizes with the animal: "Oh, he's got you fast, my beauty! . . . when he tries to ride you, don't you let him!" (142–143, omissions mine). In a short story by Honoré Willsie Morrow, one finds a similarly Aesopian use of animals to carry a double message about romance and women: A schoolmarm watches as a ranchman she loves cajoles a wild mare into submission and feels that she too is being subdued—into marriage.[19] In both instances, the muted message undermines patriarchal values with its implication that in "normal" marriage the woman is oppressed sexually (as implied by "riding") and spiritually and psychologically (as suggested by "broken").

When this bronc rolls over on Chip, the messages change. Della competently sets his fractured collarbone and subsequently plays the nurse role. Two mutually inconsistent messages appear side by side, and the present-day reader may decide which one dominates. One: In medical practice, competence and gender are unrelated. Two: Woman's proper relationship to man is that of servant, whether as doctor, nurse, or wife.

Somewhat less clear are communications about the mystery of artistic talent. Chip discovers Della's hobby of painting—lately, of painting scenes from range life—and cannot resist finishing a picture that she has begun. She perceives that his talent is superior to hers; Chip has "caught the Message of the Wilderness" (208). Presumably this message is unavailable to Della because, as a woman, she is headed for domesticity and has only parlor ambitions. A prominent politician buys one of Chip's paintings, and an artistic career for this gifted male seems a possibility (although in subsequent fiction Chip remains a cowpuncher and ranch foreman).

Chip and Della function as vehicles of projection for the author's hopes and fears about her own artistic capacity. Evidently Bower felt that she herself had caught the message of the wilderness and could somehow reconcile her role of mother and domestic servant—by the time *Chip* was published she had three children and a second husband—with that of creator of Western scenes, a talent supposedly reserved for men such as her friend, ex-cowboy and artist Charles Marion Russell.[20] Della seems to represent the author's misgivings about her own creative talent.

The conclusion of this Western romance indicates that despite her depiction of a self-reliant, professionally competent heroine, Bower intended merely to loosen without breaking the bonds confining heroines in the traditional romance plot. As closure nears,

Della's initiation into the Happy Family circle has progressed, but so has her reduction from heroine to homemaker. Chip says, "I'm going to keep you—always." Della does not protest this possessiveness, and when Chip's confidence falters—"You do like me, don't you?"—she does not even use her own language in reply; instead she borrows one of Chip's favorite expressions" "I—I'd tell a man!" The final phrase in the novel is Chip's possessive *"My* Little Doctor!" (264, original emphasis). However, the last word of that phrase implies that the heroine's reduction may not be complete; her identity as a physician and a person may not be wholly lost. The reader may equally imagine a strictly domestic future for Della or one in which she continues, even though a wife and homemaker, to practice part-time from her "office" in the ranch house. The novel, of course, had to stand by itself, but it must be noted that in subsequent Flying U fiction Della does indeed play the dual role of physician and homemaker. However, she does so only as a minor character; moreover, because the Countess does most of the housework, Della's partial freedom is maintained only at the cost of another woman's continual subjugation.

In *The Flying U's Last Stand*, the unity of the Happy Family is threatened not by romance but by an economic force spearheaded by a New Woman. Events in this novel take place seven or eight years after those in *Chip*. The economic force is the homesteaders—"nesters"—who have enclosed parts of the open range with barbed wire. The Old Man has kept the Flying U solvent, in part through diversification. Then along comes Florence Grace Hallman, field agent for a land promotion that would break up several big ranches, including the Flying U, and defraud those homesteaders who are lured into doing the actual breaking up. *The Flying U's Last Stand* is thus a novel of social protest in retrospect against the forces that were destroying the cattle-range West, including the New Woman insofar as she participated in the social and economic changes bringing about that destruction.

Miss Hallman is sexually attractive, but there is an implied masculine element in her allure. Two aspects of the New Woman image, not necessarily inconsistent, have been blended in her: a mannish "taint" and sex appeal artificially induced for business purposes. She is "tall and daintily muscular as to figure." Drawing on physiognomy, a means of characterization borrowed from nineteenth-century popular fiction, the author gives her face a detail found often in the visages of many shady males: Her eyes are too close together. Feminine aspects of her appearance suggest artificiality and therefore immorality: She wears too much jewelry and probably uses makeup. "Her eyebrows . . . were as heavy as beauty permitted," and "her lips were very red." However, with a chin that was "very firm," Miss Hallman "looked the successful businesswoman to her fingertips" (9, omissions mine). June Sochen has defined the New Woman as one "who left the home for the factory, a career, and the marketplace."[21] Miss Hallman pursues a career in the marketplace, but because the jewelry and makeup are functional in her work, they constitute a negative message about that work. She and Honoré Willsie Morrow's Miriam Page are actually combinations of the decorative True Woman and the assertive New Woman. Both are surely the sort of females George H. Lorimer had in mind when around 1901, through his persona of "self-made merchant," he complained—perhaps whined is a more apt term—that in business, "when they've got a weak case they add their sex to it and win, and . . . when they've got a strong case they subtract their sex from it and deal with you harder than a man."[22]

Concerning Miss Hallman, the chivalrous Happy Family cowpoke Andy Green feels that "a man does mortally dread" having to "fight a woman" (23), but oppose her he does. She is luring homesteaders to file claims on open rangeland, and even a few too many such claims could mean the end of the Flying U. "And that was like death," Bower writes, "indeed it *is* death of a sort, when one of the old outfits is wiped out" (21, original emphasis). Thus, even a man in Miss Hallman's position would be playing a villain's part. She of course is doubly a villain by virtue of gender and triply so because her special function as agent for "the Syndicate" is to lure women homesteaders—"daring rivals of the men in their fight for independence" (104–105)—to stake claims on land too arid for cropping.

Symbolically and with sexual ambiguity, she participates twice in the Syndicate's rape of independent women: once when she lures them onto the land and again when she tries through arson to drive them off so the Syndicate can obtain the land cheaply.

The Old Man calls Miss Hallman "that blonde Jezebel" (211). Actually, her sexual advances are confined to appearance, and Andy (Ananias) Green, himself a smooth talker and tall-tale artist, is not fooled. He shows indirectly that gender and the ability to outscheme and outlie an opponent, at least in a good cause, are not necessarily related. Inspired and guided by Andy, the Happy Family do both and the ranch is saved.

For many pages it is not clear whether or not Hallman is herself a dupe, conned by her employers into thinking she is doing right by farmers and ranchers. However, she qualifies unambiguously as immoral by hiring someone to set a range fire in order to burn out the more persistent homesteaders, including some of the women. Even so, this New True Woman exemplifies the subverted text strategy. She has at least the partial, muted supported of the author in that she definitely moves the plot and even in defeat never loses her dignity and composure. She illustrates Elaine Showalter's statement about women writers' conflicting urges:

> Even the most apparently conservative and decorous
> women writers obsessively create fiercely independent
> characters who seek to destroy all the patriarchal struc-
> tures which both their authors and their authors' sub-
> missive heroines seem to accept as inevitable. Of course,
> by projecting their rebellious impulses not into their
> heroines but into mad or monstrous women (who are
> suitably punished in the course of the novel . . .), female
> authors dramatize their own self-division, their desire
> both to accept the strictures of patriarchal society and to
> reject them.[23]

Like her creator, Hallman is a female building a career in a traditionally male field; for good or ill, she is attacking another branch of the patriarchy, the range-cattle industry. She is "suitably punished" perhaps. She has endangered lives, but none have been lost, and within the novel she is not penalized with death or with aging and consequent loss of sexual attractiveness, the punishments most often inflicted by authors of popular fiction on "bad" women. But the land promotion of which she was a part has failed, and just before the ending she takes a train out of the area and vanishes.

After the first battles of strategy and wit between Andy and Miss Hallman and before the range-fire sequence, interest shifts to the romance plot involving Andy and Rosemary Allen, one of the homesteaders. Essentially it is the romance plot that makes this novel a domestic Western. Claude Bennett, Jr. (the Kid), offspring of Chip and the Little Doctor, is six years old, and when the child is reported lost on the range, the bunkhouse sense of collective fatherhood is revealed in the frantic nature of the cowhands' search. The Kid's own reactions are also instructive. Besides his father, several members of the Happy Family have evidently been his role models. He tries to keep his cool "like Daddy Chip and the boys" (229); several times he says to himself, "by Cripes," a favorite expletive of Big Medicine, one of the Family; and he pretends he's camping "just like Happy Jack," another member. (Participation in surrogate parenthood by the bunkhouse gang characterizes other domestic Western fiction—for example, *The Little Knight of the X Bar B* [1910] by Mary K. Maule, and a set of interconnected tales about a child and a ranch crew by Cherry Wilson in *Western Story Magazine* [1930].)[24]

The search for the Kid eventually brings Rosemary and Andy together, but before that effect most of the romance plot concerns the woman's search for the child. Rosemary epitomizes the Ideal Real Woman in her ability to support herself as a homesteader and in her initial coolness toward Andy because of his reckless though humorous lying. Her combination of robust physique, courage, and capacity for analytical and imaginative thinking under stress enables her to find the child ahead of numerous male searchers. However, after Rosemary has found the Kid, she also resembles the True Woman in manipulating the boy as he tries to play man (True Women manipulate males in order to flatter their egos and get their way). When the Kid, whose macho chivalry at age six is comic as well as touching, says, "You're dust a woman—us fellers have to take care of women" (255), Rosemary controls her relief and compassion and resolves to treat the Kid "not like a little lost boy" (260) but like the "rell ole cowpuncher" (229) he wants to become. She eases his anxiety and stirs his embryonic masculinity by pretending fear of his horse.

When Andy Green finally finds Rosemary and the Kid, there is little left for him to do. Whenever she appears in the novel, Rosemary has done most of the plot-moving, thereby conveying nontraditional implications about the relative importance of women. At closure Bower bends the romance plot further by refusing to commit her heroine irrevocably to marriage: "I am not even going to tell you whether Andy succeeded in persuading Miss Rosemary Allen to go with him to the parson." She adds, "Nor whether the Happy Family really did settle down to raise families and alfalfa and beards" (352). These comments on the final page but one offer a dominant message that hero and heroine really are in love and happy, but they also include two implications from underground. One is that marriage in the cattle-range West kills male dominance and independence by demoting single punchers on horseback to farmers digging to support nuclear families. The latter is that marriage kills female initiative and strength by relegating heroines to drudgery as farm wives. This second message has been foreshadowed in a vignette about a hysterical wife with a "coarse lout" (327) of a husband.

Although *Last Stand*'s two plots—the Florence Grace Hallman plot and the Rosemary-Andy-child plot—could, with a little tinkering, stand as separate novellas, both share aspects of the domestic novel in that women rather than men are the major characters and plot-movers (most of Andy's stratagems are countermoves to initiatory ploys by Hallman). Moreover, like earlier domestic novels, this domestic Western carries underlying criticisms of a patriarchal order that is taken for granted in the overt, explicit content of the text.

In *The Phantom Herd* (1916), several members of the Happy Family have been hired to help make a Western film. By now Rosemary and Andy have married, and the male bonding that had loosened when the group accepted the Little Doctor has become even less exclusive: "Rosemary Green had been adopted without question as a member of the Happy Family" (121). On the one hand, this is a dubious honor; she becomes the servant of a number of men rather than just of her husband, and when the Family and the film producer form an independent company, Rosemary adds keeping the firm's books to her chores as cook and housekeeper for the crew. On the other hand, she plays one of the major parts in their first film. Thus, like the Little Doctor, she becomes a rarity in formula Westerns: a wife who successfully adds professional work to her domestic role.

❧

In several episodes about Happy Family member Percival Cadwallader ("Pink") Perkins, Bower voices, or rather whispers, criticisms of prevailing notions about gender. She makes Pink a means of ridiculing fiction, her own included, in which gender stereotypes are taken for granted. Basically her satirical attitude involves rejecting biological essentialism, the patriarchally sponsored view that certain behavior patterns by which gender is commonly identified are innate—that is, "natural." Pink joins the Flying U in *The Lonesome Trail* (1909). The first impression the author gives of Pink is one of effeminacy if not of unambiguous homosexuality. He is small and pink-cheeked; his garb includes a "dainty silk negligee" and "absurdly small tan shoes," and his dimples "would have been distracting in the face of a woman."[25] However, the author also invests Pink with abundant qualifications for masculinity. No doubt she wished to avoid conveying hints of deviance to the point of alienating readers and maybe her publisher, but another reason for offering evidence of Pink's masculinity was surely to stress that gender behavior is culturally acquired. Anyway, Pink turns out to be a top cowhand and bronc rider, an effective fistfighter, and a practitioner of jujitsu (173)—possibly the first martial art expert in Westerns, though far from the last. Moreover, Pink later is the first and for many years the only Happy Family member to leave the Flying U for the state of marriage—although within seven or eight months he is back in the familial bunkhouse.[26]

Along with his masculine exploits, Pink scores as a female impersonator. He is said to have fooled people once as a "lady broncho

[sic] fighter."[27] In *Rodeo,* after he has finally and regretfully left the shrinking Flying U, he "plays a woman's part" as stand-in for a heroine of Western movies, doing not only "all her stunt stuff" but also "a lot of her straight drama" (9–10). And in a piece probably written during the same period as the stories in *The Lonesome Trail* (1904–1909),[28] Pink goes to a masquerade ball disguised as a Latina or gypsy dance-hall queen and brings out the worst in masculine behavior on the part of several members of the Happy Family. Heads turn literally and figuratively, and some of the bunkhouse brethren vie for "her" attentions. Irish, who once saw the opera *Carmen,* observes the resemblance of the queen to the operatic heroine and is the hardest-hit of all the cowboys. He tries to monopolize her company as if he owns her. "Carmen" teases him and the other men until macho tension rises toward the brawling point.

Meanwhile, some of the women present, including the Little Doctor, have recognized Pink. The author implies that because of their inferior role in the power structure, women have necessarily become more skillful at dissembling and therefore at spotting that practice in men. The women quickly agree to play along with the impersonation—to support Pink, as it were, in his one-man rebellion against the conventions of gender-related behavior. Knowledge of this support, and for that matter of the true identity of Carmen, is withheld from the reader until the midnight unmasking. The reader was probably assumed to be male; whatever his or her gender, he or she is deceived along with the cowboys and thus, after the stroke of twelve, shares with them the reception of the antiessentialist message about gender traits.

Carmen's "unladylike" conduct includes laughing unrestrainedly, soliciting drinks of whiskey, smoking a cigarette—"in those days that was a serious charge to bring against any girl" (166)—and doing a shoulder-high dance kick. The Little Doctor leads the women in support of Carmen's conduct. "Isn't Rita the sweetest thing?" (163) Della asks her husband after she has seen that he is thoroughly annoyed. She even hints that she may invite the gypsy queen out to the ranch as a guest. At that, Chip, the chivalrous hero of the first Flying U novel and later a comradely husband and an avuncular figure to the bunkhouse branch of the Happy Family, becomes a potentially abusive tyrant. To borrow a phrase from Rachel Blau DuPlessis, Bower does some "writing beyond the ending" of *Chip of the Flying U* and reveals what can happen to lovers after the patriarchally oriented romance plot has ended in marriage.[29] Chip has already used force in taking Della out of Carmen's vicinity; he had "lifted her by the elbow from the bench" (162). Now he says, "I'm going to . . . lay down the law. If they [Della and a woman friend] won't listen to reason, I'll take them home if I have to tie them in the rig!" (166, omissions mine). Western chivalry remains dormant as Chip, a few minutes later, shows the prudishness that to the present day masks the possessiveness, not to say the dictatorship, exercised by many husbands. He is tempted to kick Carmen in the rear, and he says to the other Family men: "Take a slant at Irish and that Spanish— . . . giving her a name between his teeth. . . . This is supposed to be a respectable dance, and I'll be darned if I'll let my wife stay in such company. Either that girl leaves the hall, or I'll pull out with my whole outfit" (168–169, omissions mine). Within the hearing of other guests, he then bluntly rejects Della's suggestion about having Carmen out to the ranch, thus putting his wife down publicly. He does not realize that the proposed invitation was a joke.

At the midnight unmasking, tension among the males persists, as Irish insists falsely that he was never fooled, that he was only pretending to be seduced. Della and her friends exercise women's traditional function as peacemakers, and a fight is again averted. However, no dialogue of reconciliation takes place between Chip and Della.

By using the masked ball as part of the action, Bower moves her attack on essentialism and sexism into an area not often appearing in the Western, the realm of comic allegory. On this occasion Irish is disguised as a "yellow devil," and he announces that as a devil, "I'm working at my trade"—that is, of trying to dominate and degrade women. After the unmasking—a truly ironic reversal for the reader as well as for the fictional participants—Pink grins "impishly" and Chip calls him a "little devil." The incongruous shifting of the action into comic allegory has veiled but not concealed the author's implication that male chauvinism, even at carnival time, is oppressive to women.

Other costumes add to the comic element and reinforce Bower's critique. Irish's cousin Weary dresses as a blue devil, an appropriate though relatively nonaggressive role; his long-term relationship with his date, his "little schoolmarm," is cooling, and this development is indeed giving him a fit of the blue devils. Happy Jack has come as a Native American woman and fools nobody, but his impersonation nevertheless carries an imputation that even among cowpunchers, those macho embodiments of the Old West, some could have been found who were not as masculine as they pretended or cared to be. Chip has come as Daniel Boone, and this superhero disguise makes his peevish attempt to dominate his wife seem all the more ridiculous. Further, the Little Doctor's domino and the masks of the other women move Irish to declare, "All girls are mavericks tonight" (155). Two interrelated meanings are here implied and satirized. One is that men see women as strayed cattle who may be claimed as possessions by any enterprising male. The other is the still familiar notion that, without exception, when a woman says no she means yes.

Carmen's tambourine deserves attention. Literally it functions as part of the dancer's allure; symbolically, whenever she shakes it at a male or taps him with it, it represents the patriarchal notion of virginity as primarily a challenge to males. Perhaps less clearly, but at any rate plausibly, when the women try to jingle and shake the instrument, it represents an unconscious desire to break from the dominance of their husbands or dates and to emulate the daring and freedom dramatized by the gypsy queen. This interpretation is reinforced when Chip takes his wife away from her harmless jingling, with "This is no time for tambourine practice" (162). Unconsciously or otherwise, he sees the instrument as part of the threat to his paternal rule incarnated in the whole Carmen image.

"The laugh is on us all tonight" (177) admits one Flying U puncher, referring to how the men but not the women were fooled by Pink's impersonation. But in an ironic sense, the laugh is also on the women characters and on any female readers. Initially Pink's impersonation had been motivated by his desire to win a bet with Irish, but in practice his venture involves manipulation of friends and acquaintances of both genders. In his complete success with the men

The Happy Family   33

and his partial success with the women—they too are deceived, if only briefly—Pink, with his hinted bisexuality, actually is more effective in his charade than someone of completely male or unambiguously female gender could have been. Bower implies that duality of gender invests a person with more social versatility than does singularity of gender and that gender, again, is a social construct, not an innate quality.

One may also see Pink's impersonation as a symbolic projection of a male-female tension within the writer, a dissonance she kept out of most of her sixty-eight books, however she may have coped with it in her personal life. She raised four children, and her third marriage lasted nineteen years, ending only with Bud Cowan's death. Engen's statements that Bower "supposedly never married the man she really loved" (4) suggest an inner life more complicated than her public life.

As with most Westerns, a subject in the background is the establishment of civilization in the West. To Bower, as to other writers of Westerns, both male and female, civilization essentially meant domestication, but Bower's interest in depicting that patriarchally oriented process clashed with her covertly feminist slant. She partially resolved that conflict by helping to develop the domestic Western; her version of domestication was an extended family composed mostly of men who, instead of drifting on or settling down to married life, remained at a bunkhouse hearth dominated by male bonding but influenced to some extent by the wives of the two married ranch males.

Throughout the Happy Family fiction, the author stresses that in the open-range culture men were free to choose their own lifestyle. A still, small authorial voice whispers the same about women. Della's friend, Dr. Cecil Granthum, another woman physician, finds single happiness as a practitioner in the developing Montana town of Great Falls. In *The Phantom Herd*, Jean Avery Lite, helped by a tolerant husband, successfully makes a transition from ranch wife to Western film star. Jean is not an occasionally reappearing minor character like Dr. Granthum; she is protagonist of *Jean of the Lazy A*. Several single women in Happy Family fiction work land claims successfully or go into business. In addition, the depiction of a group of men living harmoniously as a family without female house- and body-servants carries the imputation that women needn't feel obligated to "save" and serve men; they too can have careers, and not necessarily as schoolteachers. Herbert Marcuse has written somewhere that those who look hard enough and selectively enough at the past may find in it elements of a hoped-for future. In looking nostalgically but critically at the vanishing cattle-range culture, Bower may also have seen a future for women more promising than they could find in nuclear families even in the rural West, let alone in the longer-settled East.

Perhaps if Bower's heroines had been more like the decorative True Woman than like the active Ideal Real Woman, and if her heroes had relied more frequently on fists and guns, the impact of her fiction on the movies might have been greater. *Chip of the Flying U* was filmed four times, but only five of her other novels were adapted for the screen.[30] By comparison, Hopalong Cassidy, a creation of Bower's contemporary Clarence E. Mulford, rode and fought through sixty-six films, on the whole eminently forgettable. That adjective should not constitute the last word about Bower's Happy Family fiction.

CAROLINE LOCKHART AND HER STRONG-WILLED HEROINES

Caroline Lockhart was an all-around frontierswoman of popular letters. During her long and eventful life she pioneered as a woman journalist, crusaded as an editor, thrived as a rancher—and wrote seven novels about the West. Of these, her first two, *"Me—Smith"* (1911) and *The Lady Doc* (1912), and the fifth, *The Fighting Shepherdess* (1919), hold the most interest for the present-day reader. Analysts of Western popular culture and students of women's fiction have tended to overlook her writings, but Lockhart deserves better. Within the Western formula she developed heroines who were variations of the Ideal Real Woman that Frances B. Cogan felt had disappeared from popular letters sometime after 1880. She also introduced a woman character type uncommon even in the "quality" fiction of the time. In addition, she vivified her work with humor and satire, most often in her contribution to what Anthony Channell Hilfer, among others, has called "revolt from the village."[1]

Besides examining these aspects of Lockhart's achievement, I will emphasize the conflict between her belief in women's freedom and her choice of fictional genre and endeavor to show how she partially resolved that conflict through the use of strategies discussed earlier in this study—notably the two-level communication of mutually inconsistent messages, the disguised projection of the author's nonconformity into unsympathetic women characters, and the creation of "women's men."

Caroline Lockhart was born in 1870, in Eagle Rock, Illinois, and raised on the family ranch near Topeka, Kansas. She attended Bethany College in Topeka and later Moravian Seminary in Bethlehem, Pennsylvania. By or shortly after her eighteenth birthday she was working for the Boston *Post*. In 1887 Nellie Bly had become the first full-time general assignment woman reporter for the New York *World*; the next year Caroline Lockhart attained similar status on the Boston newspaper and subsequently proceeded to carry out a number of unusual assignments (although Lockhart did not go around the world in seventy-two days, as Bly did in 1889–1890). By her own account, Lockhart danced in a vaudeville show, went down into Boston harbor in a diving outfit, jumped from a fourth-floor ledge to test a firemen's safety net, and wangled admission to an asylum for female "drink addicts," afterwards writing an exposé of conditions therein. Soon after that, she went to work for the *Philadelphia Bulletin,* for which she wrote features as "Suzette." During her career as a journalist, she also interviewed several celebrities, including William F. "Buffalo Bill" Cody, whose acquaintance she later renewed out West.[2]

According to Frank Boyett, one possible motivation for Lockhart's moving to Cody, Wyoming, was that "two of her former lovers were living in the area."[3] Whatever the cause, by the end of 1904 she had settled in Cody as a freelance writer. Apart from her fiction, she tried to preserve the picturesque aspects of the Old West by helping to organize the Cody Stampede, a festival that still flourishes annually. Her aggressiveness in promoting and managing this event led participating Crow Native Americans to call her "White Woman-Boss."[4]

Within eight years (1999–1919) Lockhart published five of her seven novels. She bought into the *Enterprise,* a Cody newspaper, in 1920, and three years later became sole owner. Most of her energy during this period went into newspaper work; between 1920 and her selling of the *Enterprise* in 1925, she produced only one novel, *The Dude Wrangler* (1921). Frank Boyett has written about Lockhart's political and personal quarrels with other citizens, especially Prohibition law enforcers and their supporters. As for women's rights, it is not known whether she affiliated with any of the activist women's organizations, but she promoted equality for women indirectly.

After selling the *Enterprise,* Lockhart bought a ranch. For thirty years, in Boyett's words, she "devoted her time to raising beef instead of raising hell."[5] She virtually stopped writing fiction, producing only the novel *Old West—and New* (1933) and a few short pieces. She died in 1962, aged ninety-two. Although she may have had several lovers, she never married.

Lockhart cannot be said to have written "domestic Westerns"; even so, all but one of her novels—*The Dude Wrangler* being the exception—include a plot pattern similar to that of the nineteenth-century domestic/sentimental novel. A young girl alone or nearly alone faces discouraging odds, overcomes them, and eventually finds a Mr. Right who will lead her upward along the path of social mobility and also into the oblivion of marriage and a home. This plot pattern appears even in *"Me—Smith"* and *The Man from the Bitter Roots,* wherein the protagonists are male.

Lockhart may have been the first woman writer of Westerns to make the protagonist a male villain. "Me—Smith!" is the favorite exclamation of a title character who to some extent illustrates the worst of the West. He has no redeeming quality except the courage of desperation. Even his villainy is unheroic: He is a petty horse-thief and mediocre seducer. Early in the book he murders a Native American for his blanket. Yet Smith illustrates the kind of projection defined by Gilbert and Gubar,[6] although Lockhart projects her rebelliousness into a disreputable male rather than female character. Smith feels that "to do what you aim to do and make a clean getaway—that was the successful life" (60). Symbolically, this statement comes close to fitting Lockhart herself, as person and as author. For that matter it seems appropriate for any writer aspiring to originality, especially if the aspirant is a woman writing early in the twentieth century.

Besides being a vehicle for authorial projection, Smith serves as a means of discourse on two levels. Through him the author on one level supports and on another level subverts the prevailing patriarchal ideals of femininity. For example, one convention that supports patriarchy is that men, especially heroes, dominate the tale. Smith's prominence as protagonist reinforces that view. Yet this important figure is a most unglamorous villain, and early in the narrative his effect on one woman is recalled in such a way as both to encourage and to discourage the ideal of domesticity with woman as the worshipful helpmate. Smith remembers one of his sexual conquests:

> He saw a woman seated at an old-fashioned organ in a
> country parlor. There was a rag-carpet on the floor. . . .
> Her husband held a lamp that she might see the notes,
> while his other hand was upon her shoulder, his adoring
> eyes upon her silly face. He, Smith, was rocking in the
> blue plush chair for which the fool with the calloused
> hands had done extra work that he might give it to the
> woman upon her birthday. Each time that she screeched
> the refrain, "Love, I will love you always," she lifted her
> chin to sing it to the man beaming down upon her, while
> upstairs her trunk was packed to desert him.
>   Smith always remembered with satisfaction that
> he had left her in Red Lodge with only the price of a
> telegram to her husband in her shabby purse (61, omissions mine).

In addition to a satirical view of the visual and verbal trappings of domesticity, Smith's reminiscence conveys a bundle of conventional masculine notions: Any woman can be fooled by a clever man; if her heart is faithless, she can turn the most tender expressions of love into lies; no man's hearth is safe from the seducer; therefore the utmost jealousy of husbands is simply realism. But below these messages lie others less conventional. One is that mindless adoration of wife by husband is in itself, in its unconscious possessiveness, a kind of oppression. Another is that a married woman's life—in which examples of conspicuous consumption like parlor organs, red carpets, and plush chairs are prominent—may be monumentally dull, a living death. A third message is that the decorative, romance-oriented female type (in later parlance, the True Woman) may turn out to be an unreliable marriage partner, as ripe for seduction as a wife as she had been over-ready for marriage with an unsuitable but devoted and available man.

This reminiscence also foreshadows Smith's effects on three other women, specifically his manipulation of Mrs. MacDonald, a middle-aged Sioux who falls in love with him; his unsuccessful attempt to manipulate Susie, her daughter by her deceased white husband; and his partially successful manipulation of Dora Marshall, a schoolteacher "not of the far West" (42). Mrs. MacDonald, "in appearance, a typical blanket squaw" (26), resembles the title character of Marah Ellis Ryan's *Squaw Élouise* (1892) and Annie-Many-Ponies, heroine of B. M. Bower's *The Heritage of the Sioux* (1916), in that all three become infatuated with and are victimized by white males. (These women also illustrate the convention established in nineteenth-century fiction, including the dime novel, whereby Native American women sacrifice their lives for the benefit of whites, usually white men.) Élouise is bought as a slave by the white hero, whom she loves; Annie saves the life of her white "tribal brother" by killing another white, then kills herself; Mrs. MacDonald dies after accidentally poisoning herself with a death-potion she had prepared for the deceiver Smith. In all three novels marriage between whites and Native Americans is avoided, but white racism and male chauvinism are implicitly criticized.

As the primary heroine of *"Me—Smith,"* Mrs. MacDonald's daughter exemplifies the author's use of two voices. The dominant image conveyed through Susie MacDonald is familiar. Like many of her predecessors in the domestic novel, she is young, a bit of a tomboy, fatherless, and burdened with problems created by the inadequacy of the other parent. This Ideal Real Woman has composure, courage, self-reliance, and practical competence—though only sixteen, she satisfactorily manages the ranch left to her mother by her deceased father. However, again like most heroines of the domestic novel, she ultimately gives the running of her life over to a man. The conventional reassurance is clear.

Nonetheless, in at least two respects Susie is singular rather than typical, and in that singularity lies a subsurface and socially unpalatable communication. First, she is one of the few heroines in American fiction up to that time who are part-white, part–Native American (earlier novels with such heroines include Helen Hunt Jackson's *Ramona* [1884], Ryan's *Squaw Élouise,* and Ada Woodruff Anderson's *The Strain of White* [1909]). Second, through her own initiative she several times effects changes in the plot—for example, when she robs her own mother of the money Mrs. MacDonald was fatuously planning to give to Smith and again when she unmasks Smith as a killer. These unusual aspects of Susie's image imply a socially disturbing affirmation of the humanity and rights of Native American women. Admittedly, the fact that Susie is already living as a white woman in a white-dominated society enables the author to leave unraised the problem of cultural assimilation.

Lockhart's use of the romance plot in this novel reflects the conflict between her desire to write realistically—that is, critically—about gender relationships and her choice of the formula Western as her field of writing. Essentially she incorporates within *"Me—Smith"* two romance plots, one comic, the other serious and strictly within the formula. Both plots evolve around Dora Marshall, the non-Western schoolmarm. One plot is in large part a parody of the Western romance as exemplified by Owen Wister's Virginian and the schoolteacher Molly Stark Wood. This plot is also a satire of the New Woman as reformer of cowboy manners (a type ridiculed through Alfred Henry Lewis's Cynthiana Bark and B. M. Bower's Miss Martin, a do-gooder who tries to "civilize" the Happy Family).[7] In *"Me—Smith,"* Dora and Smith make fools of each other: Dora thinks she is civilizing Smith for his own good, whereas he tries to manipulate her for his own libidinous purposes. At times he shows an affection for her other than merely physical attraction. "Am I gettin' locoed, me—Smith?" (63) he asks himself, but suspicion that he is a fool is no cure for his folly. As for the schoolmarm, "in her unsophistication, her provincial innocence, Dora Marshall was exactly the sort to misunderstand and to be misunderstood, a combination . . . as provocative of trouble as the intrigues of a designing woman" (65, omissions mine). Smith "would have been amazed, enraged through wounded vanity, if it had been possible for him to see himself from Dora's point of view: a subject for reformation; a test for many trite theories; an erring human to be reclaimed by a woman's benign influence" (118). The contrast of each character's conception of self and of the other with reality is comic in its incongruity, and the comic element is augmented by the fact that Dora escapes "happily" from the relationship.

At the very end of the novel, pathetic irony replaces comedy:

The cause of Dora's painless escape is the sudden demise of Smith. Friends of the Native American Smith killed lower him bound into a den of rattlesnakes, and his last words, motivated by courage and pride as well as by misguided affection, are, "Tell the Schoolmarm I died game—me—Smith!" (315).

In the second plot, a standard hero—Ralston, a cowboy and livestock detective—falls in love with Dora and she with him. Although in other novels Lockhart sympathetically depicts bonding between Western males, here she indicates that such bonding could do disservice to some women. The bonding unites both virtuous and villainous males and closes Ralston's mouth concerning Smith: "It would have been against every tenet in his code to suggest to Dora that Smith was not the misguided diamond in the rough which she believed him" (119). However, Dora finally sees the light about Smith, and at closure she is headed for homemaking, presumably on the ranch of Ralston's family. But after all, she is only the secondary heroine, and this "serious" romance plot could have been left out with little change in the comic, antiromantic plot, or in the villainy and foiling of Smith that constitutes the main line of action.

Before *The Lady Doc*, women physicians were still relative strangers in American fiction. During more than thirty years previous to publication of this book in 1912, only four American novels with women doctors as major characters had attracted much notice. One was Bower's *Chip*; the others, all non-Westerns, were William Dean Howells's *Dr. Breen's Practice* (1881), Elizabeth Stuart Phelps Ward's *Dr. Zay* (1882), and Sarah Orne Jewett's *A Country Doctor* (1883). Lockhart's novel differs considerably from the last three. The women doctors in those novels had faced opposition from the patriarchy, and each had also experienced a conflict between her medical ambitions and the "normal" desire to marry and to create a home and family.[8] In *The Lady Doc*, as in Bower's *Chip*, male opposition is a minor element; both authors take for granted the right of women to become physicians and their usefulness as such, at least in Western areas like northern Montana and Crowheart, Wyoming, the locale of

The Lady Doc. At the time of Dr. Emma Harpe's arrival in Crowheart, no other medical practitioner can be found within sixty miles. Moreover, conflict between medical practice and marriage does not appear in this novel; Emma Harpe's primary aims include neither conventional romance nor a domestic lifestyle.

Lockhart may have begun the novel as an indirect attack on an actual woman physician in Cody, but to some extent the project became a muckraking novel in the tradition of fiction by Lincoln Steffens, Upton Sinclair, and David Graham Phillips—exposing, in this case, the low standards and inferior graduates of some medical colleges. Indeed, one medical historian has written that "as late as 1900, there were medical schools which admitted students who could not gain entrance to a good liberal arts college."[9] Interwoven with the exposé aspect of *The Lady Doc* is the theme of conflict between the Old West and the New and the related theme of revolt from the village. As in *"Me—Smith,"* Lockhart also tries to blend critical realism with formula romance, interweaving the Emma Harpe plot with a romance that features a relatively passive hero and heroine and a rich, long-lost uncle. As in her first novel, she could easily have left out the romance plot. The omission would have made the narrative more economical without weakening its significance as a muckraking effort and as a realistic novel about the West in transition.

An interpretive summary may show the twofold nature of the action. Dick Kincaid, a prospector, finds a starving family that has been deserted by the father. Time then leaps ahead twenty years. Dr. Emma Harpe has bungled an abortion and thereby killed her best friend. (This episode may have been the first unambiguous indication of an abortion in hardcover American fiction. No message is conveyed about the morality of the operation; all that is implied is that it is dangerous when performed incompetently.)[10] Nearly thirty and unmarried, Emma flees to the West and arrives in the booming town of Crowheart just in time to advise Andy Symes, a shady promoter and speculator, to marry his gawky fiancée simply because a married man can seem more respectable in business than can a bachelor. In her social life as in her medical practice, Dr. Harpe's primary aim is to make money. For that purpose she continues to cultivate Symes, whom she sees as a rising financial star, and determines to marry Ogden Van Lennop, a rich young Easterner. There are two drawbacks to this scheme. First, Emma Harpe is a Lesbian. Second, Van Lennop is attracted to Essie Tisdale, a girl of obscure parentage who works at the local restaurant-hotel. The attraction between Van Lennop and Essie is mutual, but business draws Van Lennop out of town for several months. During that time, Emma gets Essie fired from her job. The doctor's motive is in part jealousy over Van Lennop and in part revenge for Essie's having repelled a sexual advance by her.

After Essie loses her job, the main interest in the narrative shifts temporarily to her from Emma. Lonely and destitute, Essie marries a rich but coarse and aging "sheep king." However, before the marriage is consummated, this tycoon is murdered by his sons— he was the father who had deserted his starving family twenty years earlier, and the sons have now gotten their revenge. After the murder, interest shifts back to Emma. She tries to frame Essie for the killing, but her attempt is foiled by the "Dago Duke," an Italian ex-physician and alcoholic now herding sheep. The schemes of Symes and his associates, including Dr. Harpe, to lure more homesteaders into the area than the land can possibly support are presented in detail. The schemers' main lure is a dam and irrigation project. Emma and a male doctor as unscrupulous as she is become operators of a substandard hospital financed mainly by compulsory deductions from the wages of the project workers. However, the entire project collapses because of underfinancing and mismanagement. The debacle is hastened by financial opposition from Van Lennop, although he acts primarily for sound business reasons and only secondarily because Crowheart "society" has ostracized Essie. Through interception of a letter—not exactly a new device in romance plots—Emma delays the development of Essie's and Van Lennop's mutual love, but after the hero returns to town, the misunderstanding is soon cleared up. Emma, impoverished and afraid of possible violence from mistreated workers, leaves Crowheart in the smelly caboose of a sheep train.

Emma's flight is the climax of the novel, but the anticlimactic final chapter belongs to Essie. Dick Kincaid, now wealthy, has shown up; belatedly he reveals that Essie's long-deceased parents had been respectably married and that he himself is her uncle. Actually Kincaid's role is superfluous even within the Essie–Van Lennop plot. With respect to that plot as a whole, conceivably one could justify the inclusion in the novel of Essie's fall and rise as a dramatic contrast to Emma's rise and fall. However, as already suggested, to this reader the main effect of the entire Essie plot is an enfeebling of the Emma plot through division of interest.

If the most forgettable aspect of this book is the romantic component, the most memorable is the characterization of Dr. Emma Harpe. Several of Sarah Orne Jewett's women characters play male roles, and the ambivalent sexuality of a radical feminist in Henry James' *The Bostonians* (1886) is implied with Jamesian ambiguity, but as far as I can find, Lockhart offered the first unambiguous delineation of a lesbian in hardcover American fiction (there were examples in the sensational newspaper and pamphlet fiction discussed by David S. Reynolds in *Beneath the American Renaissance*). Although Lockhart does not use the terms "lesbian" or "bisexual," she allows little doubt about Emma's sexual orientation. When weeping for her dead friend, Emma sits with "feet wide apart . . . unfeminine even in her tears." When she dresses for a wedding, she wears "a man's sleeve links;" a "man's linen waistcoat . . . added further to [her] unfeminine *tout ensemble.*" More significantly, Emma confesses to a married woman whom she finds "attractive" that "I like women anyhow; men bore me mostly. I had a desperate 'crush' at boarding-school, but she quit me cold when she married" (17, 35, 131–132; omissions mine). Emma's behavior, both as implied and as indicated directly, reinforces the impressions made by her clothing and her words. She invites Essie into her hotel room; Essie emerges abruptly with face "crimson" and says to her employer, "Don't expect me to be friends with that woman again!" (66). Later, Emma physically assaults her married woman friend "because Gussie wouldn't leave her home and go away with her! . . . Crazy! Jealous!" (337–338, omissions mine).

Yet Emma Harpe's sexual interests seem less important than her craving for money. She had selected a medical college where "the course was easy and the tuition light" (33). To Dr. Harpe, as a typical graduate of this institution, "each patient was a customer" (33); her downfall comes about mainly through her pecuniary greed. Why, then, did Lockhart make this character sexually ambivalent? Her suspicion that a woman physician in Cody was such may have motivated her in part,[11] but one need not be surprised that a woman who had pioneered as a reporter also wanted to break new ground in fiction. Further, one should consider the view of Gilbert and Gubar that female authors, by projecting their own desires into "mad or monstrous women" who are later punished, simply "desire both to accept the strictures of patriarchal society and to reject them."[12] Dr. Harpe is exposed as a medical charlatan, a common thief, a physical and moral coward, and a sexual deviant, and her future looks bleak. However, before her fall she, like Smith, has dominated the action and has influenced the lives of several less vividly depicted characters. In addition, Emma has manipulated and made fools of a number of cheats, liars, snobs, and cowards who in the main deserved what they got. The author, self-projected into Emma, has thoroughly scourged the New West element in Crowheart.

Along with self-projection into a disreputable character, the author uses the double-voiced discourse. Overtly—that is, with the dominant voice—Lockhart condemns what patriarchal society likewise frowned on, but a contradictory murmur is included simply through the gusto, humor, and suspense in those sections of the narrative wherein Emma is the center of interest. Lockhart also speaks with two voices about the role of heroines in the male-oriented Western romance. As *The Lady Doc* ends, Essie is about to marry the man of her choice, but some readers, especially women, may recall a statement she made earlier to Van Lennop about marrying a cowpuncher:

> [H]e'll file on a homestead . . . fifty miles to a neighbor
> and a two days' trip to town. . . . He'll build a log
> house. . . . He'll buy a little bunch of yearlings with his
> savings. . . . I'll get wrinkles at the corners of my eyes
> from squinting in the sun and a weatherbeaten skin
> from riding in the wind and lines about my mouth from
> worrying over paying interest on our loan. . . . Twice a
> year we'll go into town in a second-hand Studebaker. I'll
> be dressed in the clothes I wore before I was married. . . .

A dollar will look a shade smaller than a full moon and I'll cry for joy when I get a clothes-wringer or a washing machine for a Christmas present" (112–113, omissions mine).

At the end of the novel, the engagement of Essie and Van Lennop reaffirms the romantic view of marriage, but the image of the wife as oppressed party undermines that view (although the image is muted by having been expressed over two hundred pages earlier, and by the fact that Essie's fiancé is no homesteader but a wealthy capitalist).

Elaine Showalter's "woman's man" is illustrated explicitly by the Dago Duke, though primarily in a negative sense: that in law enforcement it supposedly takes a woman's man to catch a woman. Rather than blindness or injury, the Duke's handicap is alcoholism. True, he tells the baffled sheriff that "to sabe [understand] women of her sort [Emma's]" requires a Latin. "There's natural craft and intrigue enough of the feminine in the southern races to follow their illogical reasoning and to understand their moods and caprices as an Anglo-Saxon never can" (283). Surely, however, the author is ironic here; nowhere else in her available writings does one find any such stereotyped identification by the author of "southern" or "Latin" characteristics with "feminine" traits. On the contrary, it is clearly the Duke's drinking and the fact that this habit has put him down among an oppressed social group—the low-income Italian project workers—that alerts him to Dr. Harpe's manipulation and exploitation of the workers and of Essie. He sees Dr. Harpe for the harpy that she is, even though "the general feeling toward her was one of friendliness" (175) and the reaction of Van Lennop, the hero, merely "a kind of puzzled wonder" (197).

Even more than in "Me—Smith" humor and satire help to vitalize The Lady Doc. The satire is most cutting when the author compares and contrasts the Old West with the New and when she treats the theme of revolt from the village. When the novel begins, Crowheart has been invaded but not yet dominated by newcomers from the rural Midwest. At a dance, old settlers and new mingle gaily, with "no covert glances of dislike or envy, no shrugs of disdain, no whispered innuendoes The social lines which breed these things did not exist" (27). However, the "poor and the middle class of the Middle West," largely from the small towns of that area, with their narrow-mindedness, self-righteousness, and snobbery, immediately begin to corrupt this idealized bit of Old West financially and socially and are satirized through epithet, farce, parody, and incongruous metaphor and simile. Comic irony too is not lacking: For example, through their eagerness to make money by swindling workmen and home-steaders, Andy Symes and his fellow "embezzlers and ex-bankrupts" from the Midwest and East, to their eventual consternation and cha-grin, unwittingly hand over control of the irrigation project to Van Lennop, an Easterner who has absorbed the "naturalness [and] the big, kind spirit of the old [Western] days" (198).

⋈

One reviewer of *The Fighting Shepherdess* called it "a romance of a fa-miliar type."[13] Indeed, in addition to being a romance of the West, it includes elements of the domestic/sentimental novel and the novel of success. Although both the domestic and the success novel tend to feature a young person who at the beginning is a loner and a social outcast, the domestic novel differs from the success novel, even when the protagonists of both are female, in that "Success" for the heroine of the domestic novel usually means marrying a man with influence and social status,[14] whereas the protagonist of the success novel achieves prominence and affluence largely through his or her own efforts in pursuance of a career. Thus, despite their female pro-tagonists, Mary Austin's *A Woman of Genius* (1912) and Willa Cather's *Song of the Lark* (1915) may be designated success novels with as much justification as, say, Dreiser's *The Financier* (1912) and Abraham Cahan's *The Rise of David Levinsky* (1917).

In Lockhart's *The Fighting Shepherdess*, the heroine marries a prosperous rancher but not until she has won affluence through her own intelligence and resolution. The success theme and the themes of revolt from the village and of Old West–New West conflict are more deftly interrelated here than in *The Lady Doc*, and the romance plot is more smoothly interwoven with events relating to these themes. Structurally, *The Fighting Shepherdess* is Lockhart's most effective novel.

The narrative begins with Kate Prentice, at fourteen, already (to use Nina Baym's words) "deprived of the supports a girl should be able to rely on." Daughter of a roadhouse operator notorious as "Jezebel of the Sand Coulee," Kate runs away to escape sexual harassment actually encouraged by her mother. She is informally adopted by "Mormon Joe," a cultured, middle-aged alcoholic who has held himself together to the extent of owning the sheep that he herds. Kate is laughed at by children in the raw new village of Prouty, Wyoming, because of her bare feet and overalls; after that humiliation she shuns social gatherings until an educated young rancher, Hugh Disston, with whom she has fallen in love already at age seventeen, asks her to a dance. At this event, Kate's crudely self-made clothing and her unusual though entirely honorable situation as "Mormon Joe's Kate" brings about a brutal snubbing by the townspeople, especially the married women. Kate vows revenge on the whole of local society.

Later Mormon Joe is murdered, and Kate is suspected of the crime, partly because she has inherited his sheep. Starting with this band, for eleven years Kate single-mindedly builds her range holdings. During this period, she repeatedly endures further humiliation from the boomers of Prouty and their womenfolk. Eventually, as a prospering "sheep queen," she gains control of the local bank wherein she had once been curtly refused a loan.

Shortly after this milestone of self-made success has been reached, Kate's father appears. He commands capital and can turn the town's precarious boom into bust by withholding his contemplated investments. At the time of Kate's birth, he had been legally married to the "Jezebel," and Kate, reinforced by her newfound legitimacy, her self-achieved affluence, and her father's wealth—not to mention his willingness to let her decide whether the town should be made or broken—gets her long-sought revenge. She terrifies the Prouty Boosters Club and their consorts with the threat of impoverishment, then magnanimously advises her father to go ahead with investments that will save the boosters from ruin but will not make their fortunes. Kate's triumphant denunciation and forgiveness of the citizenry takes place in the same room, the social chamber of the local hotel, wherein she had suffered humiliation at the dance eleven years earlier. The author barefacedly admits that the sameness of setting is a "singular coincidence" (353). However, the irony surely is fitting enough to justify obvious coincidence this one time.

The Fighting Shepherdess contains the same conflict that pervaded Lockhart's other novels, a tension between belief in independence for women and deference to the male-sponsored norms of female gentility. For example, the author designates "sheep queens" generically as "raucous-voiced, domineering, sexless, inflated to absurdity by their success" (325), and Kate's behavior gradually comes to resemble that of these other royal entrepreneurs. Yet near the ending, after only a few weeks in a large city, she blossoms out in a "white dinner gown" and exhibits "perfect taste"—meaning the taste of the upper-middle-class True Woman—in her hair style, jewelry, and bearing. Rather tactlessly, Hugh exclaims, "Is this wonderful girl you?" (373). The reader may well share his bemusement. However, seen from another angle, Kate has shown the adaptability of the Ideal Real Woman, whereas the other female rulers of the sheep range have merely become imitation males.

Further, listening for a whisper from underground leads one to perceive how this author did in part resolve the conflict between submissive femininity and rebellious (if mainly implicit) feminism. On the surface of this tale, one finds a heroine who, after she has won her way in the world, reverts to her "naturally" feminine and passive role. Beneath the surface, a dissent is encoded in the fact that before her reversion Kate succeeds in the male-dominated world of agribusiness and does so primarily through her own willpower, aggressiveness, and efficiency. To put this message in propositional form, these supposedly masculine qualities actually are human attributes belonging to neither gender. A related undercover message: Males too may show the traditionally feminine qualities of gentleness, tenderness, and intuitive understanding. This idea is incarnated in the character of Mormon Joe, another of the handicapped—in this case, another of the alcoholic—"women's men" in Lockhart's novels.

With Kate having attained the economic and social status she seeks and having found fulfillment in romance with a (finally) understanding lover who is affluent in his own right, there seems no need to augment the heroine's well-being any further. Yet the author does so through the use of a contrivance. That device was part of the Western formula; indeed four Lockhart novels contain contrivances that are superfluous both to the ostensibly realistic lines of action and to the romance plots. In *"Me—Smith"* the Eastern guest turns out to be Susie's affluent uncle; in *The Lady Doc* the author hauls forth another long-lost, affluent relative, apparently for the same reason—to make the heroine's background more respectable according to the middle-class morality that in all four novels she also satirizes. In *The Fighting Shepherdess* up pops Kate's father; he had been married to the Jezebel and he is rich. Not only is Kate's birth legitimized, but in addition to her self-acquired affluence, she derives status and power from the wealth of her father. Earlier Kate's standards had been the "standards of the old West and of the mountains and plains, which take only personal worth into account" (53). In giving the heroine, through her father, more power and responsibility than she needs for her revenge on the townspeople, the author implicitly negates those standards. The same negation appears in Lockhart's last novel, *Old West—and New* (1933). Like Kate Prentice, Nellie Kent is first seen as a social outcast. She attains respect and security through her own efforts (in her case, as a working journalist) and acquires additional wealth and power, as well as more respect for her background, through an oil legacy discovered to have been bequeathed her by her long-deceased mother.

In the formula-Western genre, coincidences and other contrivances generally have to do with bringing hero and heroine together and punishing bad people. Why, then, did Lockhart provide heroines with extra status through contrivances more excessive than those commonly used in the genre to bring about the expected endings? The desire to give her heroines good social standing and economic power probably owes much to the author's belief in women's right to independence; however, the statement by a woman who knew Lockhart that "she was a snob plain and simple" (Hicks, 38), whatever its motivation, cannot be dismissed as irrelevant to an understanding of Lockhart's fiction.

Lockhart also shows a degree of elitism in her depiction of heroes. Five of her hero types demonstrate not only "Western" courage and decisiveness but also "Eastern" manners and taste. In *"Me—Smith,"* Ralston, a Westerner but college-trained, achieves the goal of becoming "a *man*—a gentleman" (175, original emphasis). In *The Lady Doc,* even Emma Harpe perceives that the hero, Van Lennop, is a "gentleman" (91), and something of what the author means by that term comes out in her observation that this hero "was a living contradiction of the fallacious statement that all men are equal" (118). In *The Fighting Shepherdess,* Hugh Disston exhibits "the chivalry of his good southern [i.e., southeastern] blood" (44). In *The Full of the Moon* (1914), attorney Bob Ellison, the heroine's Eastern fiancé, shows "the advantages of a trained over an untrained mind" (247), although it takes a Western challenge to bring out his potential for courage and for quick thinking. In *The Dude Wrangler* (1921), hero Wallie McPherson brings Eastern high culture with its traditional taint of effeminacy to Wyoming, where he retains Eastern manners but gains "masculinity" and thrashes an abuser of horses. This conflict between respect for Eastern education and manners and attraction toward an idealized version of Western individualism and democracy was far from new in writings about the West; it pervaded the work of Cooper and Wister and (to cite one male writer contemporary with Lockhart) the Western fiction of Harold Bell Wright, notably *The Winning of Barbara Worth* (1911) and *When a Man's a Man* (1916).[15]

If contrivance is an outdated component of Lockhart's fiction, her humor and satire remain the freshest and liveliest aspects of that fiction, especially in her versions of revolt from the village—that is, in her comic pillorying of character types from rural areas east of the Missouri. Lockhart's most effective satirical weapons are incongruous metaphor and simile. A regrettably brief sampling: Of one spindly Easterner it is said that "his legs look like the runnin'-gears of a katydid" (*"Me—Smith,"* 20). A newcomer to Crowheart dances "with the darting ease of a water spider" (*The Lady Doc,* 28). Another migrant from Eastern parts "looked chaste, if somewhat like a wind-mill in repose, in her bridal gown" (*The Fighting Shepherdess*, 42). In the same book a Prouty boomer with hair "sleek, glossy, fragrant, brushed straight back" looks like "a muskrat that has just come up from a dive" (358).

Data on the reception and sales of Lockhart's novels are sparse, but a few clues indicate that her first three may have sold more than a few copies. *"Me—Smith"* was published in February 1911, and at least two more printings were made during that year, although how many copies were printed cannot be determined. *The Lady Doc* stirred controversy in and around Cody[16] but seems to have aroused little interest elsewhere. *The Fighting Shepherdess* may have attracted the most popular attention of any of Lockhart's books. Within weeks after its publication, a fourth printing may have been issued. Again, the number of printings indicates little about the actual sales or the number of readers, but in 1920 a film based on this novel was produced; Anita Stewart, a star in early "silents," played the title role.[17]

Notices of Lockhart's books were few but generally favorable. Two reviews praised the author's attempts at realism in *"Me—Smith."* One wrote that "as a delineation of western life at once realistic and picturesque it compares favorably with Mr. Wister's 'The Virginian' "; the other, evidently no fan of Westerns, called the book "a tale of the Wild West sufficiently plausible to deserve reading by grown-up persons."[18] A reviewer of *The Lady Doc* wrote aptly that "the artistic flaw in Miss Lockhart's work [is that] she has mingled with a popular tale of the more ordinary type of western story a character which demanded more subtle setting and treatment."[19] A commentator on *The Fighting Shepherdess* praised the author's "absolute sense of truth"; another designated this novel "an interesting story of the West."[20] Lockhart's books may have equally disappointed readers looking for an action-packed romance in the manner of Zane Grey and those who expected the verisimilitude of a Theodore Dreiser or the character-probing of an Edith Wharton. There may have been too little of the Western formula in Lockhart's work for one class of reader; for another, too much.

Lockhart's fiction, at least the three novels discussed herein, deserves resurrection for several reasons. First, her heroines are among those Ideal Real Women who, one might say, migrated from the domestic novel into the formula Western. True, Essie Tisdale and Kate Prentice deviate from the "real" type by behaving rashly about marriage—Essie weds a sheep king, and Kate, in a fit of despair at ever winning Hugh Disston's love, takes the "unladylike" initiative of proposing marriage to her foreman. However, Essie's husband is murdered, Kate's foreman sensibly rejects her proposal, and both heroines subsequently behave like rational, self-possessed Ideal Real Women.[21] Second, Lockhart created a major character who was probably the first unmistakably lesbian figure in Western formula fiction and one of the first in American fiction in general. Third, overall Lockhart's fiction transmits a subtextual message inconsistent with the dominant communication. Her "loud" voice asserts that women with the right stuff marry and become invisible homemakers for the heroes. Her "soft" voice insinuates that in the Old West, a strong-willed woman could find freedom and challenge outside of marriage and that for such women even marriage might not mean total depersonalization. A corollary: To women as well as men the Old West offered the freedom, even the right to make mistakes. Dr. Harpe is punished for hers, but Essie and Kate are allowed to participate in "happy" if conventional endings. Fourth, Lockhart showed herself adept at irony and satire, especially concerning village mores.

Lockhart chose the formula Western as her mode of writing but rebelled against the sexism built into that formula. Her modus operandi deserves further attention not only for what it reveals of how one feminist author coped with a set of macho conventions but also because of the freshness and readability her novels retain even today.

VINGIE E. ROE'S NOVELS
OF BESET WOMANHOOD

Many readers thought that Bertha Muzzy Sinclair Cowan was *Mr.* B. M. Bower. Even if Mrs. Virginia Lawton's pen name of Vingie E. Roe had not strongly suggested feminine gender, surely few readers of more than one or two of her novels could have made an equivalent mistake about this author. In Roe's work one finds an early twentieth-century feminist—sans ideology—who, having chosen as her field of achievement the formula Western, manipulated the genre in part by using strategies already employed by some women writers but not yet articulated in propositional form. Nina Baym has written that much American fiction boils down to "melodramas of beset manhood," and Joanna Russ has listed a number of stereotyped, male-originated images of women in popular fiction—the "virgin victim . . . the faithful wife, the beautiful temptress, the seductive destroyer, the devouring mamma, the healing Madonna." Russ says, "None is of the slightest use as myth to the woman writer who wishes to write about a female protagonist."[1] Owen Wister had seen the cowboy hero as a reincarnation of the knights of old. Almost as if she had set out to revise Wister's concept, Roe invested her heroines with knightly attributes, blended these attributes with those of the Ideal Real Woman, and put the characters into melodramatic novels of beset womanhood.

Between 1912 and 1957, Roe's output included at least thirty-one novels in book form, most of which feature active, plot-moving female protagonists that remind this reader of Britomart, the female knight in Book III of Edmund Spenser's poem *The Faerie Queene.*

57

Armed, armored, and invincible in combat, Britomart symbolizes Chastity, and in Spenser's Renaissance version of the romance plot, she looks forward to predestined marriage with Sir Artegal, an allegory of Justice.[2] Several of Roe's heroines do indeed marry lawmen, and more than a few are elevated by analogies with mythical female figures. Belle Dawson is "Valkyrian"; nineteen-year-old Lacey Caloran is a "young Juno"; rancher Nance Allison is a "young goddess"; logger Elsa Jensen a "belted Amazon"; a certain homesteader's daughter is "like a wild dryad"; and Bryce Hayward is called "Blue South Woman" (wife of the sun god). That designation is also given Dr. Sonja Saverin by her Navajo patients, and Sonja's white suitor calls her a "white angel in armor." Sabine of the "Great Valley" is a "golden goddess."[3]

Knightly or not, most of Roe's heroines function effectively in traditionally masculine roles. Some are leaders either of families with absent or defective parents, or of groups larger than nuclear families. Several run ranches, for example, the heroines of *Tharon of Lost Valley, The Divine Egotist,* and *The Silver Herd,* also the villainess of *Nameless River.* At least five heroines are the formal or *de facto* leaders of entire communities: the heroines of *The Maid of the Whispering Hills, The Splendid Road,* and *The Teamstress* lead wagon trains; the title character in *Black Belle Rides the Uplands* is initiator and leader of action by the ranchers of a considerable area, and the heroine of *Smoke Along the Plains* heads a group of homesteaders. Though not leaders, some of Roe's women are charismatic activators within their respective communities, such as the heroine of *The Heart of Night Wind,* a force within her adopted Native American tribe, and the protagonist of *The Golden Tide,* the outstanding figure in a group of single women pioneers.

Evidence that Roe was an overtly feminist ideologue is lacking; indeed, most of Roe's heroines tend to fall in love at first sight and in that respect resemble the images of True Womanhood found in some nineteenth-century domestic fiction. However, in their self-reliance, physical fitness, and multiple skills (riding, shooting, roping, and plowing, as well as the traditionally female skills of cooking, nursing, housekeeping, and child care), Roe's heroines, like those of Caroline Lockhart, exemplify the Ideal Real Woman of the pre-1880s and seem to owe little to the Hurricane Nells of the dime novel.

In only one of Roe's late novels, *The Golden Tide* (1940), does an authorial interest in women's rights as a social movement appear to any considerable extent. However, through the larger-than-life heroines of her fiction as a whole Roe implies women can and should do everything that men can do and that they can do it without ceasing to be female. She told an admirer that "in all my yarns it is I who ride all the horses, shoot all the guns, kiss all the handsome heroes."[4]

The view that women can take men's places in even the most "masculine" pursuits receives nearly explicit formulation in a short story that features a lone woman who, aided by her dog, kills a panther and puts up a notice: "Here's where White Ears the dog and Lola killed the panther. Our mark."[5] Thus had Daniel Boone left a "famous inscription that 'D. Boon Cilled a Bar.'" Lola implies that she has taken the place of Daniel Boone as protector of the home. In an earlier story, Lola traps White Ears, who is really half-wolf, nurses him to health, and tames him "with love."[6] In the sequel cited above, she moves easily from a domestic role to that of provider and protector—and back again: The panther injures White Ears before she can dispatch the menace, and she reverts to her function as the dog's nurse and care-giver. This "superwoman" (the author's term) has successfully played both male and female roles.

In some respects Lola is a simplified version of characters more fully developed in this author's longer fictions. Like Lola, the heroines in Roe's novels show by example that women can equal men in significant ways without losing their womanliness and becoming either mere imitations of male character types or specimens of male-originated female stereotypes. However, within the two Lola short stories Roe omits the romance plot and thereby avoids the problem that tested her in her novels, as it had tried Bower and Lockhart—the convention that romance must end in marriage and the disappearance of the heroine into domesticity. This chapter will largely concern how she coped with that problem.

✎

Virginia Eve Roe was born in 1897 in Oxford, Kansas, daughter of a physician and an "ex-school-marm."[7] The family moved to Guthrie,

Oklahoma "when I was just beginning to recognize my kinship to dogs and horses."[8] This kinship was externalized in her fiction, from the "mammoth mongrel" hound and the stallion Black Bolt in *The Heart of Night Wind* (1913) to the Appaloosa horses of the heroine Johnny Jim in *The Silver Herd* (1957). In Roe's case, life matched popular fiction; Daryl Jones has pointed out that the rapport of "good" humans with animals was common in dime novel Westerns.[9]

Of herself during her teens, Roe said later, "I was a tomboy and an enthusiastic Methodist at the same time. Many a reluctant youth did I drag to Epworth League in those days."[10] These statements harmonize with her later interest in religion, an interest manifested in the tendency of her heroines and some of her heroes to mingle biblical phrasing with the language of love and, in a few cases, with invocation of specifically Christian values, a tactic unusual in the formula Western.[11] For instance, the hero of *Flame of the Border* refers to his relationship with the heroine as a "Soul's covenant," and she echoes, "Soul's covenant . . . from everlasting to everlasting. Amen."[12] Similarly, in defying the villainess, the heroine of *Nameless River* draws spiritual reinforcement from the Psalms.[13]

Roe once told a reporter that she had left school in the sixth grade "because she didn't like the multiplication table and she did like her pony 'White Eagle' and freedom and the out of doors."[14] Later she came indoors long enough to enroll in a rhetoric course at Oklahoma Agricultural and Mechanical College (now Oklahoma State University) taught by Angelo C. Scott, then president of the college, to whom she dedicated a late novel, *The Great Trace* (1949). At the age of nineteen she encountered another inspiring figure. Roe's father had been a friend of Heck Thomas, a noted Oklahoma lawman, and Virginia recalled later that "it was a romantic high-light to me when Heck Thomas gracefully unbuckled his gunbelt and laid it and its two white-handled guns on my mother's center table. And thrill of thrills—he let me hold them in my hands a moment!"[15]

She married Raymond C. Lawton in 1907, and some time before 1911 the couple moved to Oregon, where they lived near the isolated lumber town of Toledo (the setting for the *The Heart of Night Wind*) and later near Medford. Still later they resided in northern California.[16] Few details about the Lawtons' married life relevant to the fiction of Vingie E. Roe are available. She told an interviewer that she devoted mornings to writing before preparing lunch for her husband, but "he sweeps and makes the bed. . . . He is a helpmate of the first degree."[17] However, sometime after 1918 the Lawtons were divorced, and Virginia lived with her mother until the death of the latter. No children are mentioned in any available sources. One relative has implied that conflict between Roe's mother and husband caused the breakup and surmises that Roe "loved both" but chose her mother because the latter was "the underdog, the helpless one."[18] Whatever Virginia's motives concerning the divorce, in several of her novels written after that event, the prospective marriages of hero and heroine at the endings contain, as will be seen later, the seeds of their own dissolution.

Roe's beset heroine is often dark-eyed, black-haired, and swarthy or olive in complexion. Roe herself was said to have had "purplish-black hair and Irish-blue eyes,"[19] a combination found in several of her protagonists. Whatever the author's personal motivation, her consistent presentation of "dark" heroines reverses the tradition of fair heroines and dark villainesses. Says Daryl Jones, "Dime novelists frequently portray the temptress as a fiery and passionate woman of Latin blood."[20] Roe's Britomart is fiery and passionate— but chaste. Often she is of French, French-Canadian, or Hispanic ancestry.

How does the Roe heroine function in specific contexts? Three of this author's novels will be examined in detail: *Nameless River* (1923), *Black Belle Rides the Uplands* (1935), and *The Golden Tide* (1940). In *Nameless River*, the author pits two superwomen against each other. One has strongly religious motivation, which, like the woman vs. woman contest is uncommon as a central theme in formula Westerns. Of the other superwoman, Roe writes:

She was a gallant woman, not large but seemingly built
with such nicety of proportion as best to show off the
spirit in her. Under her sombrero, worn low and level on
her brow, one seemed to see darkness shot with fire-black
eyes and dusky hair above cheeks brightly flushed. She
rode at ease. . . . As the blue horse sidled expertly down

the slope, a loose stone turned under his shod hoof, causing him to stumble ever so slightly, though he caught himself instantly. As instantly, the woman's spurred heel struck his flank, her swift tightening of the rein anticipated his resultant start. "Pick up your feet, you!" she said sharply (Part One, 8, omissions mine).

Experienced readers of Westerns surely noted the unnecessarily severe treatment of the horse and guessed that this woman would not be the heroine. Any such predictions were accurate.

"Two strong women battle for supremacy in the early West." This is one of several plots that Joanna Russ suggests would not go over in our male-dominated culture because "the sex of the protagonist has been changed (and correspondingly the sex of the other characters)" (3, 4). Yet, Russ's sentence comes close to summarizing the main story line of *Nameless River*. In this novel, as in Caroline Lockhart's *The Lady Doc*, the protagonist is a female villain, Kate Cathrew; her antagonist is Nance Allison, one of Roe's few blue-eyed, blonde heroines. Kate runs a large ranch, "riding herd after them [her cattle] like any man, branding, beef gathering, her keen eyes missing nothing" (Part One, 32). As for Nance, since the murder of her father she has done the planning and the plowing for the Allison homestead. Kate tries to kill Nance with a rifle shot at long range and later orders one of her men to throw a knife through her window; Nance scribbles an appropriate verse from the Bible, sticks it on a knife, and hurls it back toward the thrower. If, as Anne Falke has said, "the whole structure of the Western depends on opposites,"[21] Roe has followed the formula—except in the matter of gender.

The Allisons are not nesters but small-scale ranchers. Cathrew is a big-scale rancher—and rustler—who covets for cattle feed the choice flats that Nance is farming. Thus the struggle between two strong women is augmented by the conventional ranch story (which includes "rustlers versus ranchers") and with the avenger story, which "concerns the relentless pursuit of the evildoer by a Nemesis."[22] In combining the three plots, Roe, again, is keeping the narrative within the formula.

To some extent Roe has made the evildoer a Morgan le Fay

under a sombrero. With a dress "cleverly shaped to set off her form . . . she [Kate] was either a fool or very brave, for she was the living spirit of seduction" (Part One, 32). The wanted criminals who work for her do so mainly because jobs on this bona fide ranch offer refuge from the law; even so, Kate demonstrates a power over them virtually witch-like. For example, when she quirts the brawniest of them, "his red-rimmed eyes were savage with rage and hurt, but behind both was a flaming passion of admiration." A bit earlier: "No doubt there were hot hearts in the outfit who desired to make her theirs, but she passed one and all in her supreme indifference. Rio Charley carried a bullet-scar in his right shoulder, and Big Basford walked with a slight limp—yet they both stayed with her." This enchantress who has inflicted injury to repel lechery has also "got good work out of them [the lechers]" (Part One, 32).

A confrontation demonstrates which of the two women is the stronger, physically and mentally. Kate tries to quirt Nance, who grabs her wrist with "a hand which had held a plow all spring" and proclaims that "the hand of God is before my face and you can't hurt me—not lastingly." She does not, however, turn the other cheek but swings the other woman, "whirling like a dervish, clear to the middle of the porch." Kate runs for her rifle; the sheriff says accurately, "That woman's a maniac for the moment," but succeeds in cowing Kate with the threat of justice (Part Three, 59).

Meanwhile, a nemesis has shown up in the person of Brand Fair, a mysterious drifter with whom Nance falls in love. Ignoring the possibility that the six-year-old boy with Brand may be his illegitimate son, Nance and her mother agree that Brand can be trusted—"He's different" (Part Three, 15). For more than half the novel, the chief movers of the action have been Kate and Nance. But now Brand Fair and the sheriff discover the cave-tunnel through which Kate and her gang rustle cattle out of the area, and an Easterner named Arnold arrives at Kate's. It is revealed that although Kate Cathrew is the sole operator of the ranch, Arnold is half-owner and Kate's paramour. "You do need another head [i.e., a man's] to handle this," Arnold tells Kate concerning Nance Allison's refusal to give up the flats (Part Five, 31); he then proceeds to mishandle the situation. He, not Kate, has Nance kidnapped and delivered to one of their henchmen for torture and rape. To this brutal moving of the plot Kate functions as a mere accessory and Nance as an object—apparently. The next morning, the villains find "a tragic wreck of a woman whose garments hung in fantastic shreds upon her body . . . over her from head to foot was blood." Nevertheless, in this episode Nance is more of a plot-mover than at first appears. A man lying nearby when Nance is found clutches the left side of his face, and a passage follows which appears in the book but not in the version serialized in *McCall's Magazine.* " 'Gone!' he cried hoarsely, 'gouged slick an' clean! An' she tried to get 'em both—damn her hussy's soul!' "[23] In preserving her honor, Nance has literally tried to scratch the man's eyes out and has halfway succeeded.

The males provide the main action one more time. Brand Fair shows up with a posse, rescues Nance, and announces that Arnold and Kate had robbed a firm in the East and framed his (Brand's) brother for it. He adds that the boy is Kate's offspring by the now-deceased brother and therefore is rightful heir to the ranch. Kate moves the plot to its conclusion; she tries to shoot Brand and ride off but is killed by the horse she has so often mistreated (Part Five, 43).

The depiction of Kate offers a good example of the two-level discourse. An obvious and commonplace message conveyed through her is that theft, murder, and adultery will receive due punishment in this life. However, in this character are incarnated at least four ideas that are unconventional as well as covert. One is that a woman can manage a ranch as efficiently as can a man, even with unruly and unstable male personnel (Nance also works a farm and ranch, but she employs no help). Another is that if a woman can do what Kate does, surely she could perform effectively in other roles traditionally reserved for men. Kate uses sex appeal as one means of controlling her punchers, and from this fact one gets the third message: She is only imitating male employers who do likewise to control women.

A fourth message concerns male classification of women. Although Kate has had two lovers and borne a son by one of them, more emphasis is laid on her commission of the same nonsexual crimes perpetrated by most male villains in Westerns—rustling, land embezzlement, robbery, murder, and general misuse of power. No extenuation is offered for Kate's adultery, but a hint is conveyed that, contrary to patriarchal criteria, morality and immorality in women consist of much more than their being sexually of the "right" or "wrong" kind.

The messages sent through Nance are less easy to split into overt and covert communications. Endemic in popular fiction is the idea that hard work and perseverance are part of any winning combination of virtues. Unmistakably Nance incarnates this view, but whether the rest of her winning combination is religious or secular in origin is unclear. Nance feels that her support comes from the God of the bible; she reads Scripture every evening, and her answer to one threat on her life is invocation of Psalms 27:1—"The Lord is the strength of my life; of whom shall I be afraid?" In reply to her crippled brother's implication that he would defend the Allison ranch with gunplay, Nance quotes Psalms 23:4—"Thy rod and thy staff they comfort me"—and adds, "We have no need of guns" (Part One, 32). However, when she is kidnapped by Kate's men, her initial feeling is the wish that she might be gripping her late father's rifle; the prayer she then utters is only her second response (Part Five, 32). Further, near the ending, when Kate, foiled and cornered, takes a shot at the hero, Nance sincerely tries to kill her, and the motivation of saving the life of the man she loves is tainted by a desire to do violence, which has been a family tradition: With her father's gun now in her hands, she is "a daughter of the feudal mountaineers who had marked her Pappy's line" (Part Five, 38). Kate's long-mistreated horse throws her, causing both shots to miss, and the horse then tramples the villainess to death; of this turn of events the author says, "And here the hand of Destiny reached down—or was it the hand of God!" Thinking she has killed Kate, Nance cries, "I am forsaken of my God" (Part Five, 38, omissions mine). Reassured that she did not kill, she confesses that she had tried to kill the would-be rapist whose eye she had gouged. Shortly thereafter, in reference to justice having been done that day, a minor character says, "It's Destiny." Nance answers, "It's the hand of God."

Nance's conscience is finally clear, but the author, having posed a question in which she contrasts a secular conception of destiny with the biblical concept of deity, advertently or inadvertently refrains from answering that question. Unresolved too is the implied question of whether the intent to kill, even in defense of an innocent loved one, is justifiable on biblical grounds. Roe's raising of these issues without exploring them further suggests an unresolved conflict within the author between the morality of Scripture and the code of violent justice basic to the formula Western. Roe's projection of this conflict into the heroine also suggests that Jane Tompkins's comments on "Christianity's striking absence from the [Western] genre" and "the Western's rejection of Christianity"[24] seem oversimplified, especially when applied to women writers in this genre. Besides *Nameless River*, Frances McElrath's *The Rustler*, Honoré Willsie Morrow's *Judith of the Godless Valley*, and Forrestine Cooper Hooker's *The Long, Dim Trail* are Westerns in which aspects of Christianity receive considerable attention.

Roe's projection of part of herself into a sympathetic woman character is expected; less so is her self-projection into the villainess, though that too should not surprise anyone familiar with Elaine Showalter's comments on projection by women authors. Kate, even more than Nance, exemplifies female entrepreneurship in a male-dominated field—as did her creator. In *Nameless River*, Roe composed a novel that, along with Caroline Lockhart's *The Lady Doc*, filled a gap in the history of the formula Western. Many male authors projected themselves into more or less sympathetic villains as well as into heroes and thereby experienced vicariously the freedom to do evil as well as good. At least one woman author projected herself into a male villain: Caroline Lockhart In *"Me—Smith."* In *The Lady Doc*, Lockhart also offered a villainess as protagonist; Roe joined her in that rare practice. Roe may or may not have known Lockhart's work, but she must have felt that if male authors could enjoy the sort of vicarious freedom just indicated, so could a female colleague and competitor.

A fairly common theme in Westerns by men is the "civilizing" of a lawless, violent male character by another male. The civilizer is usually a top gun on the side of law and order—for example, Clarence E. Mulford's Hopalong Cassidy, Henry Wilson Allen's Wyatt Earp in

Who Rides with Wyatt? or the Lone Ranger and Matt Dillon in any number of radio and television episodes. In *Black Belle Rides the Uplands* (1935), Roe gives this theme a reverse bend by having Belle Dawson, the female protagonist, oppose the law and order represented by an honest sheriff (as do the heroines in *Tharon of Lost Valley* and at least two of Roe's short stories).[25]

If only one of Roe's novels could be discussed here, *Black Belle* would be a good choice. Nearly every quality found in most of Roe's heroines appears in Belle. A female protagonist who outdoes men in traditionally masculine pursuits, from leadership (of men) to gunplay, she also vibrates with sex appeal, functions effectively as nurse and frontier paramedic, and runs a ranch, yet supervises household chores competently enough to show promise as a future wife and homemaker. She also moves the plot crucially, invites comparison with mythical superwomen, and has an inner problem with the pride of power, a problem found commonly in heroes rather than in heroines of the Western. The only aspect of some of Roe's heroines that Belle does not share is the role of foster mother to small children.

The spell of this heroine extends beyond the home ranch. Men in the area avow that she is as "good as any man in man's work and square dealing" (5) Half the bachelors around have proposed to her; she has "laughed at them all," but "it was significant of her and of her power that they were still her friends" (34). When she rides the range, followed by her pack of hounds, "the girl, the stallion, the running dogs" make Sheriff Stan Ansell think of "Amazons and huntresses and fabled women of the past" (15). In her competence both outdoors and in, she resembles to some extent the Ideal Real Woman of the domestic novel.

A dutiful daughter, she manages the ranch only because her father is weak, though not in character—a bullet from the Jake Yager gang of rustlers has left him an invalid and mentally clouded. Belle longs to avenge her father, and her feelings are intensified by the simultaneous attraction and repulsion she feels concerning Yager. Like Val in *Val of Paradise* (1921), Sandra De Halt in *The Splendid Road* (1925), Cymbaline in *Sons to Fortune* (1934), and Copper Ann Kincaid in *West of Abilene* (1951), Black Belle can play cards as shrewdly as any man and does so in that masculine preserve, the saloon. During one card game, Yager harasses Belle, and she hits him hard with her fist—something Maron LeMoyne in *The Maid of the Whispering Hills* (1912) and several other Roe heroines also do to men with overaggressive hands. Nevertheless, Yager announces that Belle is "my woman" (41), and he seems "so sure, so certain, so possessive, that Belle Dawson felt the flesh creep on her body. . . . She was a murderer that moment in her soul" (56–57). Functioning as civilizer, Sheriff Ansell prevents Belle from shooting Yager and warns that she is acting not out of vengeance but "for vanity" (64). After Belle has inspired other ranchers to meet rustler violence with violence, Ansell accuses her of having "started a cattle war . . . regardless of the law" (46). Indeed (the author interpolates), "she had started one, all because a man had laid a freckled hand on her shoulder" (48–49). Belle shows almost as much pride and willfulness as Kate Cathrew of *Nameless River.*

However, Belle sees herself "pledged to a cause as truly as a knight of old" (72)—say, a Britomart—but for awhile, her zeal distorts Ansell, in her view, into one of the villains: She "hated him as bitterly as she hated Yager" (120). Jealousy and pride, seen here as evidence of immaturity, have set Belle's heart against her head. She spurns Ansell's request for help in rescuing a young woman held prisoner in the rustler's roost, feeling that the sheriff wants to tie her hands "by giving me a common cause about some hussy that probably likes her place" (100). But she also begins to hunt on her own for objective evidence of Yager's crimes. About them, "she knew in that heart of hers as well as she needed to know, but she was manjust, man-sane in her judgments, and she must have proof" (133). Belle's psyche includes a woman's heart and a man's capacity for reasoning—a traditional split in popular fiction—and the author's point is that elimination of the split is not only possible but necessary for development of the individual as a whole. Belle's drama thus becomes one of beset womanhood maturing beyond the constraints of gender to personhood. Yager is the stereotyped attractive brute—Stanley Kowalski under a Stetson—who threatens to widen the inner breach between a woman's heart and head; Ansell, no less virile, is gray-eyed Justice (Sir Artegal), helping to heal the breach with the assistance of a belated and as-yet unrecognized ally—the mutual love developing between hero and heroine.

That love is again tainted by jealousy when Belle sees Ansell lurking around Yager's place with an unknown blonde female. Mainly to help rescue Yager's woman captive, Ansell has sent for Rose Ivory, a dance-hall queen who on occasion works as a federal deputy. She manipulates her way past Yager into his stronghold, and she and Ansell rescue the captive—who is no hussy and who abhors her "place." Belle then moves the plot from crisis to climax. From her father's incoherent mutterings she has deduced that he once planted in the cliff above Yager's canyon a charge of explosive sufficient to start a landslide that would seal the canyon completely. In the showdown, Belle detonates the explosive just in time to catch Yager in the canyon and to save the life of Ansell. In so doing she kills her arch-enemy—and her repressed attraction to him. In having no moral scruples against killing in the line of duty and in actually fulfilling that duty, Belle has taken the place of the traditional hero no less than has Lola, the female Daniel Boone. Also no less than Lola, in killing she has protected her home. She thus reflects, as does the freewheeling law-woman Rose Ivory to a certain extent, the conflict between traditional female preferences and the rebellious urge to imitate and outdo males that pervades Roe's work—and, in varying degree, the Western fiction by most of the other women writers introduced in this study.

This is not to say that killings by heroines were frequent in the formula Western. In Roe's thirty-one novels there is only one other such capital action—by Tharon in *Tharon of Lost Valley*—and in the novels of other women writers discussed or cited in the present volume there is only one more, in B. M. Bower's *The Heritage of the Sioux.* Among male authors, Zane Grey, James B. Hendryx, Nelson Nye, and Henry Wilson Allen each let at least one heroine step into the traditional male role of executioner, but in thus amending the code of the fictional West these authors were exceptional.[26] That code requires that any killing by a "good" character must preserve honor and save lives. In the climactic sequence of *Black Belle,* the heroine's honor is in no danger, but she does save the life of the hero; Yager is armed and almost certainly intends to shoot the sheriff from ambush. Belle also appropriates the masculine role of honorable avenger; she avenges the crippling of her father.

In *Black Belle,* Roe does not depict female jealousy and possessiveness as these feelings were often represented in popular fiction— that is, as inevitable components of a woman's love. Instead, she depicts them as defects that must be exorcised by reason functioning in harmony with love—by the head and heart in mutual reinforcement—if one is to attain full personhood. The same attitude pervades other works by this author. In an early short story, Roe shows a woman's unchecked jealousy as part of a deterioration of personality that leads horribly to murder and insanity.[27] In *The Splendid Road,* heroine Sandra De Halt conquers jealousy, gives up her "Sir Galahad" to the woman he is already engaged to, and thereby finds inner peace (A tacked-on, conventionally happy ending brings the hero, now a widower after three years, back to her door).

Not as integrated emotionally as Sandra, Black Belle is unjust to Yager's captive, and about Rose Ivory, she says to Ansell, "Take your cheap woman. You've got your types mixed up. I'm not her kind" (236). After Ansell has explained his purpose in using Rose Ivory's assistance, Belle still has trouble with her inner self. "For a long time Black Belle Dawson stood in silence, her dark head bent." Finally, she says, "Forgive me, Stan" (275), but after the lovers have clinched, she can't resist asking Ansell if he loves her better than his duty. His reply to this question is: "You should not ask it" (276). Evidently he will continue as sheriff against her wishes, and this apparently happy ending thereby includes an embryonic conflict. For the present, Belle will presumably go on running the ranch, sharing homemaking chores with her mother, who earlier gets a two-level authorial comment: "It seemed that always this little fair woman was either just coming in or going out with her burdens of replenishment for those who worked and ate prodigiously" (90). The overt message here reminds us that homemaking can be drudgery; an even more critical but less obvious communication is that in the patriarchal view only men's work may be rated prodigious; women's homemaking may be just as much so, but men take it for granted.

A significant authorial comment about Rose Ivory—"Ansell had called her 'notorious and capable' . . . and had fallen far short of her due. She was an artist lost to the world. . . . She could have swayed audiences, played on emotions, been famous and rich, had she been a little more ambitious, not quite so lazy" (201, omissions mine). The author has individualized Rose by blending the stereotyped shady-lady-with-a-heart-of-gold with another type, the talented but immature and failed artist, and by making Rose an arm of the law. According to the Western formula, she must be punished for her loose lifestyle, and she is: She doesn't get the hero, and although paid a "wad of money" for her successful mission with Ansell, she winds up "back on the Border" (274). Nevertheless, the author has for a few pages projected part of herself into Rose, as in *The Heart of the Night Wind* (1913) she had done with Poppy Ordway, another career woman (a writer, no less) who had erred morally. Further, insofar as they are more vivid and compelling characters than any of the men in either *Night Wind* or *Black Belle,* Poppy and Rose convey an underlying message encouraging rebellious and creative individualism on the part of women.

When the author is female, the creation of a woman as self-reliant and as charismatic as Belle, and for that matter as most of Roe's other heroines, is in itself a covert rebuke to the patriarchy. Making her the protagonist of a formula Western compounds the criticism, as does having the heroine rescue the hero (which Belle does by bringing the cliff down on Yager). In *The Rescue and Romance,* Diana Reep points out that most rescues in romantic plots are of women by men and that the convention of rescue "dictates absolute standards of behavior for men and women and reinforces the accepted, traditional roles and relationships of the sexes." That is, "when a man rescues a woman he gets the woman as a prize, but if a woman rescues a man she is apt to get nothing." Why? "Because it is not natural for a woman to rescue; it *is* natural for men to rescue."[28] Belle's rescue of Ansell implicitly denies both notions.

Roe's rebuke to the patriarchy includes the message that courage, independence, and resourcefulness are gifts bestowed equally by the Creator upon women and men and that if women will make use of these gifts, they will break the bonds of gender and live fuller lives. The same message is relayed by archvillainess Kate Cathrew as well as by Poppy, Rose, and some of Roe's other flawed women. The corollary is that although these women have sinned, they should not (so whispers the subversive voice) automatically be considered the "wrong kind"—even though, by the rules of the genre, they are ineligible for marriage with the hero.

∾

Roe's *Wild Harvest* (1941) features an unmarried woman homesteader who in 1889 is called—inaccurately—by a man, "One of these Women's Rights females" (87). Similar direct allusions to women's social and political efforts are rare in Roe's novels—except in *The Golden Tide* (1940). In this work the author bends and twists the Western formula to produce a narrative that is in part a historical commentary on woman's role as civilizer in the West and a rejection of her role as a commodity with no rights or personality. The dominant message in this text affirms and supports woman as both civilizer *and* commodity. However, the insinuated message is a critique of how the patriarchy forces woman as civilizer to collaborate in assuming and internalizing the more degrading role of commodity. Although *The Golden Tide* exemplifies the domestic Western, it differs from Bower's Happy Family novels in that female bonding replaces the primarily male bonding depicted in Bower's domestic narratives.

Historically, a thirty-four-year-old widow Eliza Farnham, concerned about the absence of women among the gold-seekers of California, tried in 1849 to organize a band of "intelligent, virtuous and efficient women" for emigration thereto.[29] The enterprise died early, but *The Golden Tide* is in part an imaginative projection of what might have happened had the plan been carried out. "Mother" Elizabeth Farnham (whose resemblance to the historical Eliza Farnham ends with the name) has collected forty-two adventurous and single young women and chartered a ship to take them to California, where they will "hold such a marriage mart as no one had ever heard about" (14). The girls "would be no man's pickings, either, for they were all provided for, since every girl had been obliged to bring her own passage money and a certain amount over and above." Moreover, they would live together and would also go into business sewing and cooking—"at stiff prices of course" (14).

One of these women, Lancie Burfield, exhibits an unfeminine independence. She shocks the fatherly ship captain by declaring, "I wish I were a man" (16), and defies his ban on women going ashore "in that hell-hole of the seven seas [Panama City]" (17). The formula is followed when, on shore, she falls in love at first sight with Shardford Benton, likewise bound for California. A second case of love at first sight occurs as the ship pulls away from the wharf at Panama City: Susan Brent, who will become Lancie's closest friend, and a gold-seeker on the pier kiss their hands to each other, and she promises to wait for him in California.

Soon Farnham's group is advertised thus in the California mining town of Red Shirt:

Marriage Market
Forty-two young ladies. All able to cook. All virtuous. All desirous of finding decent husbands. (No others need apply.) Also no hurry. No girl will marry without due courtship and knowledge of applicant. Strict formality observed. Rigid decorum and courtesy demanded. In the meantime there will be for sale on Tuesdays, Wednesdays and Saturdays, doughnuts, mince pies and cakes. Mending done neatly, on clean articles only. Plain sewing, shirts, scarves, handkerchiefs. Prices high. Bible reading and hymn service every Sunday in the yard. No callers except on days mentioned. We are respectable, self-supporting and mean to stay so (88).

Had Frances B. Cogan's terminology been in use in 1849, the advertisement could have indicated that in their caution about marriage, their intent to turn their domestic skills into business assets, and their independence (even if this is envisioned as only temporary), the subjects of the ad see themselves as Ideal Real Women rather than as True Women.

Mother Farnham, who wrote the notice, acts out the contradiction between helping women to civilize the West yet dealing in them as a commodity. She and her "girls" do deviate from paternalistic capitalism in making their project to some extent a collective endeavor; even so, the Marriage Market is accurately recognized as competition by the only other female-run business in town, the Crystal Hall. This establishment includes ten women managed by Black Rose, "young in years but old as Methuselah in questionable wisdom" (89)—though unwise enough to fall, again in accordance with the formula, hopelessly in love with gambler Monty Breed.

Soon Lancie begins to sell something on her own. She has an outstanding singing voice and prefers exercising it at Monty Breed's saloon to sewing and baking. Consequently, when Shardford Benton shows up, romance between Lancie and Benton is complicated by his unchivalrous but understandable notion that she has become Breed's fancy woman.

Lancie does regularly send part of her earnings to Mrs. Farnham and the group. Mrs. Farnham wishes to reject the profits of disloyalty and possibly of immorality, but the girls affirm their faith in Lancie's character and vote to accept the money. Sisterhood knits most of them even more strongly when two are lured into the Crystal Hall and there forcibly detained. Lancie's friend Susan proposes a raid; one woman objects. Another says, "They're just our little sisters—the babies of this outfit." Susan becomes an aggressive big sister: "In two minutes Susan had whaled her [the objector] to a howling pulp" (153). The "swarming herd of Amazons" turns the interior of the brothel into "heaps of ruin" (156)—one thinks of Carrie Nation and her saloon-wreckers—and the overawed whores peacefully surrender the two girls in a rescue episode, the second of its kind in a Roe novel (and a kind not found by Diana Reep in her investigation of rescue and romance).[30]

Already the formula of the Western historical romance has been bent to include collective female domesticity, and the reshaping is not over yet. True, some events do fit the formula. For instance, twice in the novel, prostitutes play the healing-Madonna role, the second time when Black Rose, whose jaw has been broken earlier by Monty Breed, uses the discarded splints for that injury to bind up his bullet-shattered hand—"the same hand which had smashed her—and was humbly grateful for the chance to serve this man" (173). However, this female victim and servant later kills him (and thereby becomes a plot-mover).

74   Vingie E. Roe

Certain other developments are less formulaic and send provocative messages from the underground. For example, Susan has found her lover-at-first-sight weak from typhoid and totally destitute. She has prospered in the sisterhood, but she tells Lancie she will "heal his hurt pride" and never let him know she has money "until he makes enough to match it. We'll start even in all things" (234, 235). On the surface, her attitude constitutes an inspirational example of love, loyalty, and understanding, but below, one senses the resentment of the author against a social order that encourages resourceful and self-reliant women to pretend that men are sturdy oaks and they themselves merely clinging vines. However, the fact that in a male-dominated culture the two cannot in any sense start "even" is not hinted at by the author. Her rebellion has limits.

Other events that stretch the formula concern the fate of some of the minor woman characters as the "long house" collective gradually diminishes in number. Most of the women make or still expect to make promising marriages, but a few plan instead to do "various things, like going back east with the gold they've made, or starting in businesses for themselves" (228). One becomes the mistress of an Englishman posing as an aristocrat who deserts her and leaves her penniless, whereupon the sisterhood takes her back in. Of the two women rescued from the bordello, one voluntarily returns to the establishment. Lancie is glad that the other is "safely married" (229), even though the husband is the pimp (naturally he is not called that) who earlier had lured both women into the Crystal Hall. Again Roe reveals the limits of her rebellion.

Within those limits, subsurface dissent is definitely conveyed through all these events and may be summarized briefly. Most if not quite all women thrive on freedom, but in a genuinely free marriage market a majority of women would still choose conventional marriage, and most of these would pick their mates wisely. In general, even though some women might make unwise choices, they deserve the same freedom, the same right to take risks and make mistakes accorded to men. As for the very few women who might choose promiscuity, who and what encourages that conduct and even makes it a business if not the patriarchy? Finally, female bonding enhances both extended sisterhood and each woman's worth as an individual.

Beset Womanhood   75

Another set of developments in which the formula is strained concerns Lancie—her past, her ambition, her future. To expedite her career as a singer, she manipulates Monty Breed by allowing him to build a hall in which she gives successful concerts under his management. "He's never meant anything to me but money" (191), she tells a doubting sister. Actually, Lancie has all along been married—in a loveless match to an elderly man from whom she has run away. Her husband suddenly confronts her, having, as he says, "come half round a world to find her." Lancie admits that "I sold myself to—John—for clothes and money—for position and for the chance to sing—in Paris," but simply could not live with him. "He was so hard and cold and cruel—and he was old" (247). The author tips the moral balance in her favor by making the deserted spouse a repellent character. In husband John's face the fatherly ship captain sees a "bland and iron-hard egotism" (247), and John reasserts his possessiveness with "sudden, vicious wrath" (248).

When John lays "one of his thick white hands" (249) on Lancie, Breed shoots him dead—thereby setting her free—and is himself killed by the jealous Black Rose. During this climax the author keeps the hero, Shardford Benton, passive, thereby reducing his stature—probably to encourage more reader support for Lancie at the end. Though she has become formally engaged to the well-to-do Benton, making a home for him plays a strictly indeterminate part in her plans. "Smiling, her hands folded over his, she turned and looked toward the . . . toward life, and Panama, and—France (251, omission original). They will be married in Panama, but to Lancie, France means further study toward a career as a singer. A message is encoded in the unconventional diction, punctuation, and broken syntax of the above sentence: Lancie may have sold herself for a second time, and for the same reason as the first. With this message comes yet another: The social order so thoroughly discourages careers for women that a female with talent and ambition who sells herself in marriage in exchange for means to pursue professional success deserves our sympathy if not necessarily our approval. By deserting her first husband, Lancie has broken two interrelated rules of the patriarchy: that the husband has absolute rights over his wife's body, and that the wife's preference for a career over homemaking is

76   Vingie E. Roe

immoral and socially unacceptable. The author covertly indicates approval of these breaches by killing off the first husband and by having their perpetrator marry a well-to-do spouse who is also young and robust. The romance plot is carried to its conventional conclusion only in part; the ending also implies endorsement of Lancie's giving her career a high priority even though her fiancé's feelings about that priority remain unknown.

In *The Golden Tide*, Roe tried to present an idealized woman's collective and to dramatize women's problem of career versus home while staying within the formula. What she produced was a fictional rarity: a blend of formula Western and utopian novel; a domestic Western with an extended family held together by female instead of male bonding. Further, the overt proclamation, a bit unusual but socially acceptable, that in gold-rush times marriage in the West could open new freedoms for Eastern girls is weakened by the whisper that marriage, East or West, often was and maybe still is a disguised, genteel whoredom.

Happy endings in Westerns by women often encode some criticism of the patriarchal ideal of marriage, and the less-than-happy endings noted in this chapter amount to subversion of that ideal. Besides *The Golden Tide*, four of Roe's other novels have endings in which the heroine settles for a future husband who is not the man she loves most intensely; the man either does not know or accepts the fact that he's the heroine's second choice. In *Wild Hearts* (1932), the man knows and accepts; in *Woman of the Great Valley* (1956), he may or may not know; in *Sons to Fortune* (1934) and *Wild Harvest* (1941), he definitely does not know. Writes Roe of the heroine in *Sons to Fortune*—"So well had she loved once, so deeply had she known its transports, that she could feign it now. Would always feign it" (306). In each case Roe tampers with the romance plot—that "trope for the sex-gender system as a whole"[31]—and thereby implicitly rejects the masculine ideal of complete loyalty and total submission of wife to husband.

In *Wild Hearts*, a Native American woman tells the heroine that women give all and men "give back nothing," yet life for a woman isn't life unless it includes a man and children (115–116). This contradiction pervades Roe's novels and therein is never resolved. Why not? One comes back to the conjecture that, having been inspired by visions of the Old West and having decided to make a career of writing fiction, Roe chose to write within the Western formula but was not wholly comfortable with her choice.

In coping with this contradiction, Roe in several ways resembled other women who wrote Westerns, but in a couple of respects her approach differed from theirs. Rather than being forlorn waifs, most of Roe's heroines are already established as leaders of a family or a larger group at the beginning of the narrative. In addition, Roe augmented the heroic and mythical aspects of her heroines by giving a new twist to a frequent tactic of male authors—namely, including the hero's horse among the males to which he may be bonded. For example, Jim Silver charges through at least ten novels by Frederick Faust (Max Brand) on Parade,[32] and in the visual media William S. Hart and Fritz, Gene Autry and Maverick, Roy Rogers and Trigger, and of course the Lone Ranger and Silver were famed human-equine combinations. In Roe's fiction, besides Belle Dawson and Bright Arrow, combinations of heroine and horse include Siletz and Black Bolt (in *The Heart of Night Wind*), Jane Gleason and Grey Hawk (in *Wild Hearts*), and Belle Stannon and Starwing (in *Dust Above the Sage*). In most of Roe's novels the Man on Horseback has been unseated by the Woman on Horseback. Moreover, because all of this author's supersteeds are stallions, her Britomarts have figuratively married their mounts. If this neo-Freudian speculation has any degree of validity, the horses are rivals of the heroes as well as another means of adulterating the romance plot. At the close of every novel in which the heroine-horse bonding occurs, the heroine keeps her horse; the hero, at least symbolically, does not unseat her. Instead, he must share her with the animal and thereby relinquish the traditional male right of total possession of "his" woman.

❧

At the present time Roe, like Lockhart, remains virtually unknown even to students of popular culture.[33] It should therefore be no surprise that reliable sales figures for her novels seem to be nonexistent. The scarcity and coolness of reviews of her novels suggest that none of them challenged the best-sellers of their respective days,[34] although in February 1912 the author asserted that her first novel, *The Maid of the Whispering Hills,* had already "gone through its first edition of 10,000 copies."[35] Seventeen years and at least seven novels later, she wrote that "I have made my own living for twenty years"[36]— in the main, presumably, by writing fiction. Her income from the motion picture industry may from time to time have significantly augmented that living. According to one source, a film based on *The Maid of the Whispering Hills* was directed by Western star William S. Hart, who also acted in the picture; the same source asserts that Hart and Roe "were close friends ever afterwards."[37] Hart also directed and starred in an adaptation of *The Primal Lure* (1916). Films based on *The Splendid Road* and *The Golden Tide* appeared in 1925 and 1953, respectively, the latter under the title *The Perilous Journey*. At least two of Roe's short stories were also adapted for the screen.[38]

Though her allegiance was divided between feminism and success in writing Westerns, Roe criticized male-oriented values and propagated a feminist view of women's rights and roles in the mythical West—and by implication elsewhere. In this twofold motivation she resembled the other women writers introduced in this study. Her style, barely alluded to herein, was definitely her own, for better or for worse. (One reviewer was turned off by Roe's "exasperating and quite ungoverned style.")[39] At best, the prose of this author carries the reader along with gusto; at worst, it descends to gush. Because of their substance and because—or possibly in spite of—their style, the works of Vingie E. Roe deserve recognition and understanding rather than the oblivion into which they have been allowed to fall.

WOMEN, RELIGION, AND POLITICS IN THE WESTERN NOVELS OF HONORÉ WILLSIE MORROW

Such notice as Honoré Willsie Morrow has received from scholars has concerned her historical novels rather than her Westerns. Ernest E. Leisy felt that her Lincoln trilogy, *The Great Captain*, showed "some sentimentality" but was executed "with a sense of drama and with a great deal of reality."[1] (The longest and most ambitious of Morrow's works, the trilogy included the novels *Forever Free* [1927], *With Malice Toward None* [1928], and *The Last Full Measure* [1930].) According to one encyclopedia of literature, "The name of Honoré Willsie Morrow brings to mind a number of earnest, painstaking, well-documented American historical novels"; her writing of Westerns is merely mentioned. In another such compilation one finds favorable comment on *The Great Captain*, and allusion to the fictionalized *Mary Todd Lincoln* and the nonfictional *The Father of Little Women* (about Amos Bronson Alcott), and a mere listing of her other novels. An obituary notice in the *New York Times* bore the headline: "Honoré Morrow, Writer on Lincoln."[2]

In varying degree, seven of Morrow's novels contain elements of the formula Western and merit study of how, with or without conscious intent, the author strove to express feminist inclinations within this genre. The seven also show how she used the double-voice strategy to offset and extend the limitations of the genre. Of these seven novels, three hold additional interest for analysts of popular culture. In *The Heart of the Desert*, the white, Nordic heroine marries a Native American hero; in *Judith of the Godless Valley,* major emphasis is placed on the relationship of religion to sex, marriage, the family, and evolutionary theory; and in *The Exile of the Lariat,* encouragement is offered to political action by women. Thus, in each of these three novels Morrow presented material and attitudes uncommon in early-twentieth-century Westerns by women—or by men.

⌇⌇⌇⌇⌇⌇⌇

Born in Ottumwa, Iowa, in 1880, Honoré McCue graduated from the University of Wisconsin and, like Mary Hallock Foote, went West with an engineer husband. For several years the then Mrs. Willsie strove to combine impressions of the Southwest and the people she met there with elements of the formula Western. Moving back East, she edited a women's magazine, *The Delineator,* from 1914 to 1919, publishing, among other Western pieces, two short stories by Vingie E. Roe. She also continued to write fiction, first as Honoré Willsie, then, after her divorce and her second marriage, in 1923, to William Morrow, as Honoré Willsie Morrow.

With her first novel, Honoré Willsie became, so to speak, a pioneer in Western romance writing. C. L. Sonnichsen has asserted that before Jane Barry's *A Time in the Sun* (1962), a Native American male could not, in fiction, fall in love with a white woman and survive: "To aspire was to expire."[3] However, in 1909 a regional publishing house brought out *The Brand: A Tale of the Flathead Reservation* by Theresa Broderick, in which the white, Nordic heroine marries a hero who is genetically one-fourth Flathead, although he lives a white lifestyle as a prosperous rancher. Three years later, B. M. Bower's *Good Indian* and Willsie's *The Heart of the Desert* were published. In the former novel, the heroine marries a hero who is one-fourth Sioux; in the latter, the white heroine from the East gives her heart and hand to a full-blooded Native American whose genetic mix—Apache, Mojave, Pueblo—suggests that he represents the Southwestern tribes as a whole.

In *The Heart,* one way in which the author manipulates the Western formula is simply by making a woman the main character. Another way is her use of the rescue theme. Diana Reep has stated that a rescue is usually of a woman by a man, that it controls the romance plot, and that it "reinforces the accepted, traditional roles and relationships of the sexes."[4] In the opening sequence of *The Heart,* Charles Cartwell, whose Mescalero Apache name is Kut-le, performs a definite if not spectacular rescue in applying first aid to reduce the heroine's suffering from the sting of a scorpion. Reep says the rescue of a woman by a man usually means that eventually the hero will get the woman as a prize, and so it proves in this novel. Having fallen in love with Rhoda Tuttle, Kut-le undertakes to rescue her from herself; this effort provides most of the narrative. Thus a conventional pattern, rescue of woman by man, leads toward the unconventional ending.

Rhoda's parents have died suddenly, and she has slipped into a progressively apathetic state that in the nineteenth century would no doubt have been termed neurasthenic. So far, this visit from her home in the East to friends in the Southwest has done her no good. Kut-le kidnaps her and forces her to spend many weeks with him and three Mescalero companions, two of them women, in the desert. He hopes that his prize will be a woman restored to health by this experience (which does not, of course, include sexual molestation). He assures her that "I will make you well before I marry you" (47). Even as the desert and its people are indeed making her well, Rhoda's loathing of Kut-le for his forcible abduction gradually changes to a feeling of mingled hate and love. Eventually her growing love overpowers her hatred and neutralizes her horror of miscegenation.

By the time these changes have occurred, Rhoda herself has effected two rescues, neither of which follows conventional patterns. Friends, including John DeWitt, her former fiancé, pull her from the Indian's clutches, but DeWitt will not get his hoped-for prize. He and Rhoda become lost in the desert, and the physical endurance and will to survive that Rhoda has gained through her previous desert ordeal make the difference between survival and death; she saves both her own life and Dewitt's. According to Reep, convention dictated that in rescue of a man by a woman, unless the man was already in love with her, the woman remained emotionally unrewarded because rescue of a man by a woman was "unnatural" (172). However, Rhoda does not want DeWitt's love. Later she rescues another man by convincing DeWitt that she really does love Kut-le just in time to prevent DeWitt from shooting him dead. In this case, the rescuing woman proves her moral worth and gets the man she loves as prize. The author has manipulated two elements in the Western formula, kidnapping and rescue, and eventually has given the woman a role more active than that of a merely passive victim of abduction.

In bending the Western formula Morrow has also modified the traditional romance plot, and at closure she changes that plot still further. The hero makes plans to spend one or two years in Paris with his bride, which implies that return to the Southwest and his work—and her assumption of the homemaker role—are put off indefinitely. (Ignored is the future problem of bringing half-blood children into a world wherein they might face greater difficulties even than those encountered by full-bloods.)

In altering the romance plot, Morrow has also used the double-voiced discourse strategy in reverse. Through the outcome she obviously signals opposition to the prevailing disapproval of Indian-white miscegenation. However, for years the hero has lived the life of the whitest of whites, so to speak—he graduated from Yale and has achieved status and affluence as an engineer. He returns temporarily to tribal ways solely to rehabilitate Rhoda and win her love, and there is no question but that the couple will live as upper-middle-class whites. Thus, instead of presenting a dominant, conventional message undercut by implicit rebellion, Morrow makes the unconventional message the dominant one; the reassurance that miscegenation is not even conceivable unless both parties are *culturally* white slips across only through the details of Cartwell's adopted past and of his future lifestyle and plans. True, another low-key message is the rebellious imputation that miscegenation is conceivable at all, and still another is the controversial insinuation that nurture outweighs nature—that in the shaping of character, culture is more important than heredity.

In addition to composing variations on the rescue theme, Morrow bends the Western formula in one other direction, perhaps to make the unusual romance plot acceptable to a broad readership. In themselves, certain formulaic elements in *The Heart* are relatively little changed—for instance, the superior physique and hardihood of the hero, and his prowess as a rough-and-tumble fighter (he has two fights, in one of which he subdues his rival, DeWitt). However, his being an engineer rather than a cowhand or saddle tramp exemplifies another trend then new in Westerns: the rise of the engineer as hero.[5] This trend may also be seen in the engineer protagonists of Morrow's *Still Jim* (1914) and *The Forbidden Trail* (1919).

Sequences involving flight and pursuit are of course common in Westerns, as are those depicting the challenge and influence of wild nature. In *The Heart of the Desert* this influence is related to two other ingredients of the formula. One is the education to maturity of an Easterner through experience with the West. Among other effects, this experience turns Rhoda from a merely decorative True Woman into an Ideal Real Woman. Before her sojourn in the desert, Rhoda "had never worked with her hands. . . . The most violent housewifely task that Rhoda had ever undertaken had been the concocting of chafing-dish messes at school" (109, omissions mine). In the desert she becomes "expert at camp work" (199), including fire-making, cookery, and Apache-style basket-weaving. Inwardly, Rhoda experiences an emotional rebirth in which Kut-le functions as a surrogate father and teacher. She falls in love with the desert; Kut-le is "the heart, itself, of the desert" (273). One chapter is entitled "Entering the Kindergarten"; another, "The First Lesson." Kut-le presides over her practical education as well as her emotional development.

The other formulaic element related to wild nature as education and therapy is the tendency of the West to bring out the worst as well as the best in each individual. Morrow gives the formula an unusual twist. When Kut-le and DeWitt fight, DeWitt, the representative of Eastern elegance and cultivation, does battle "like a cave man" (267), trying to kill, as he lusts to do earlier and almost does later. Instead of having the Western hero enforce the law of fist, gun, and rope, Morrow has the Easterner trying to do so. The Westerner fights for a more humane goal: to subdue his foe without killing or breaking any other rules of civilization. Even his forcible but gentle abduction of Rhoda has a humane and moral purpose. In fact, one more staple of the romance plot in *The Heart* is the hero's belief that fate has brought him and his ideal woman together.

In addition to the ancestry of the hero and his rescue by a woman, yet another element in this novel uncommon among contemporaneous Westerns is the strong if brief protest against white brutality toward Native Americans. One of Rhoda's friends cites the torture and murder of his brother and sister by Apaches; Kut-le retaliates by telling how whites murdered his mother and two sisters and scalped a third, age three, alive.

An element rare in Westerns by men but frequent in those by women is the antipatriarchal message conveyed through minor characters and their interaction with major figures. One such message is implied in a dialogue that begins after Alchise, an Apache male, yanks Molly, one of the Apache women, over backward by the hair. Rhoda is indignant and so is Kut-le—until he learns that Alchise had offered violence not to Rhoda but only to Molly. He tries to cool Rhoda's anger by saying, "Indians are pretty good to their women as a general thing. They average up with the whites, I guess" (95). Throughout the desert sequences, Kut-le orders the women about like the servants they actually are, subtly but clearly illustrating that in both white and Native American cultures men not only dominate but brutalize women. Rhoda may find her future husband typical in that respect, and this implication makes Kut-le's later oration about women ring hollow: "Life is a simple thing, after all. To keep one's body and soul healthy, to bear children, to give more than we take" (126). Rhoda does not reply, but "we" surely refers to women. Concerning women's role as childbearers Molly earlier comments, "Work, have papooses, die. That all squaws are for. Great Spirit says so. Squaw's own heart says so" (121). Molly's inability to bear children and her consequent low status in the tribe tinge her statement with bitterness, a feeling possibly shared by the author. In the novel *Still Jim* and in several magazine articles, she joined those commentators, male and female, who worried about the low birth rate among New Englanders and their descendants by comparison with that among southern and eastern European immigrants. Yet Honoré remained childless; she and Henry Willsie eventually adopted a boy and two girls.[6]

The Heart received six printings during the year of its publication and later inspired a movie, *The Red, Red Heart* (1918).[7] Morrow followed this book with three more set in the Southwest, all with male protagonists and none with any aspect as strikingly unusual as one finds in *The Heart*. Even so, the heroines in two of these novels are more active than those in most Westerns by males. In *Still Jim* (1914), Penelope Dennis is no Progressive Era New Woman, but she does agitate among ranch wives to get their men to support the hero's irrigation project. She also, again on her own initiative, intercedes in person with the secretary of the interior in Washington and thwarts an attempt to take the hero off the project, thereby changing the plot fundamentally. Muted but definite in her actions is the message that women should disregard patriarchal mind-stamping, upgrade their self-images, and use their potential for independent thinking more fully in their private lives and in their public lives—as aggressively melioristic a message about women as one could put into a Western without turning it into a novel of social protest. In *The Forbidden Trail* (1919), the heroine homesteads with her brother and works in the fields like "a pioneer's mate." Like Rhoda Tuttle, she evolves from True Womanhood to Ideal Real Womanhood: The onetime "happy-go-lucky college girl" lays aside her "white frock" and becomes a "mature, sun-burned, wind-blown woman" (103, 226). Ultimately she will make a home for the hero, but her outdoor labors, not to mention her midwifery at the birth of a Native American baby, imply that if necessary she could get along quite well on her own.

According to one source, Honoré Willsie's husband encouraged her to write. In an article about the Willsies' adoption of children, the author referred to her husband only as "the boss" but admitted "A man married to a female fiction writer has his own side of the story!" ("The Adopted Mother," 660). These bits of material could hardly be considered evidence of a rift between Honoré and Henry had they not surfaced in 1922, the year of the Willsie's divorce. However, a short story published in December 1921, "Breaking the Blue Roan," shows an affirmative yet critical view of women's role in conventional marriage roughly similar to the attitude implied by Morrow in *Still Jim* and *The Forbidden Trail*. Edith Acher, a schoolmarm from the East, admires a wild mare and accurately associates the ambition of Western men to break the animal with arrogance toward women. The attitude of the mare's owner is simply, "She's a beauty and she's got to be broke!"[8]—meaning that she must be broken precisely because she is a beauty. John Hardy, a rancher with whom Edith already is in love, begins the breaking of the mare with symbolic verbal stroking: "The best fun in life for horse or man is the saddle." After this bit of soothing confusion—who, after all, is in the saddle?—he subdues the mare with a maximum of patience and a minimum of force. Subsequently Edith, who has a history of harmless somnambulism, rescues the horse from theft while walking in her sleep. John proposes to her, and she says "I've always hated the thought of marriage so! But . . . I guess you've broken me with gentleness, too" (16, omissions mine).

Clearly Edith identifies with the mare. The thief would have broken the animal with brutality, a process that, according to part of the dominant message, a stout-hearted woman should and will resist subconsciously as well as consciously. More of that message (for the times, a liberal but socially acceptable communication): Women should reject attempts at force on the part of men and should insist on the "gentleness" that is a large part of real love; they should risk marriage only if they are sure of the prospective husband's gentleness. But the muted message, conveyed through the symbolism of breaking a horse, is that marriage, with or without gentleness, involves breaking the spirit of the wife—a subversive criticism indeed. In Bower's *Chip of the Flying U*, essentially the same muffled comment on breaking the female spirit is conveyed as Della watches Chip bust a bronc. Chip's horse is male, but Della calls the animal a "beauty" and thereby implies an analogy with women.

Honoré Willsie's grandfather had been a Methodist circuit rider, but her mother had turned to Unitarianism, and the future author experienced what one commentator called a "godless childhood." As late as 1917 Honoré referred to herself as an "agnostic," but during the next ten years or so she developed a belief that reconciled the biblical God and biological evolution; she also became a regular churchgoer.[9] However, she followed convention by pretty much keeping religious topics out of her Western fiction—until *Judith of the Godless Valley* (1922). Into this novel she put her growing interest in Christian faith and its relationship to marriage and to women's roles in general.

Judith Spencer, a tomboy of fifteen when the book opens, eventually decides that marriage, rather than destroying true love, will reinforce it. In her case, it offers the challenge of working with her husband to bring an interdenominational community church into Lost Chief, an appropriately named frontier settlement in the northern Rockies. In other words, she will accept the conventional female role of wife and civilizing force in the West. Meanwhile, however, Judith, as a girl developing into womanhood, is as beset with hardship as most heroines in nineteenth-century fiction. Her father is long dead; her stepfather oppresses her mother and unashamedly lusts after his stepdaughter. The abused mother asserts, "No one who hasn't been married can possibly understand men, or fear them or despise them, like they ought to be feared and despised" (30). Small wonder that Judith questions the whole institution of marriage. She feels that it oppresses women with an unnatural choice: If a girl marries, she's supposed to become "like Mother" (65), one of the "right" kind of women whose normal lot is brutalization by the husband; if she doesn't marry, she will become the "wrong" kind of woman, as exemplified by Inez Rodman, the town whore and bootlegger. Inez Rodman is a typed prostitute-with-heart-of-gold who, says Judith, has "given me more sensible warnings about men than my mother ever did" (165). With "all the sadness of sixteen" (78), Judith argues with Douglas, her stepbrother, about marriage, sex, death, and morals. On one occasion Judith challenges Douglas to define what he means by good. The double standard, and chivalry as represented by Tennyson's Sir Galahad, get into the conversation:

> "Well, I call being good not drinking or stealing or being loose with men or any of those things—for a girl."
> "And for a man?" asked Judith, sitting erect.
> "Aw, who wants a man to be good?" laughed Douglas.

"I do," replied Judith, with a sudden thrilling intensity in her young voice. "I want his strength to be as the strength of ten, because his heart is pure" (102–103).

Douglas vows to be "good" in that fashion, whereupon Judith asks him to give up his petty cattle-rustling. Douglas insists that this is not badness but "business." Later, Judith helps another boy do some rustling and finds that "If Doug runs cattle, he's admired. If I run cattle, I'm punished!" To which her stepfather's reply is, "Doug's a boy; you're a girl" (111). The obvious message: Like it or not, women must accept the double standard. The covert communication is critical if not exactly subversive: Women should not like it and should at least try to change men's minds.

Motivated by his love for Judith, Douglas helps a few of the townspeople build a chapel. A "sky pilot" of indeterminate affiliation, the Reverend James Fowler, is induced to begin a ministry in Lost Chief. The author makes neither a hero nor a hypocrite of this clergyman; instead he is something of a bumbler, embodying the idea that goodness may appear in ordinary and even comic guise. He does not recognize the oppression of women as a problem in itself; he is reduced to name-calling about the skepticism of one abused wife—"This is blasphemy!" (23); and he denies that the Song of Solomon contains any sexuality. Worst of all, his "sermons were dull" (262). However, he is warm-hearted, and he observes shrewdly of Lost Chief, "It's a transplanted New England community, and people who come from Puritan stock can't get along without God" (275).

After Fowler has preached a sermon denouncing Inez Rodman as the local "Magdalene," a group of men, most of them married, run him out of town. Judith's stepfather is one of the leaders, and Judith, hysterical, decides the time has come for her to leave Lost Chief forever, which she sets out to do even though a blizzard is raging. With help from a Mormon ranch couple, Douglas saves her life in a conventional rescue, but Judith still refuses to consider marriage to him because she "cannot bear to think of killing love by marriage" (327). Douglas comes back with platitudes about "marrying decent women" because "race instinct" turns a man toward "something better than himself for his mate." Judith suspects "an excuse for the double code." Douglas never does renounce that code explicitly, and on this occasion he replies to Judith, "I'm just stating one of the selfish, brutal facts of life" (334). Douglas is trying to break the blue roan, disguising, even from his self, the brutality of male domination with his version of gentleness. On her part, just by voicing her suspicion about the double standard, Judith implicitly undermines it.

Fowler, who has returned to Lost Chief, assures Judith that the community offers much opportunity to a woman with a brain and the right kind of vision. She could, among other things, make it a "paradise for children." Judith muses, "I never did believe there was a God. But that's not saying He's not to be found if you really hunt for Him." The supernatural essence "we young folks are looking for" (346–47) includes the idea of possibly divine-sanctioned physical and spiritual growth as expressed in a poem by W. H. Carruth, from which Judith quotes: "Then a sense of law and beauty / And a face turned from the clod, / Some call it evolution / And others call it God" (347).[10] A moment later, she urges the minister, "Let's go home with Douglas and get to work!" By work, she means rebuilding the chapel the mob has destroyed. But before that job is begun, Judith and Douglas are married by the Reverend Mr. Fowler, and Judith's future as a ranch wife and church worker is assured. She wants children—"I'd love to have half a dozen babies" (326)—and she now believes that with marriage will come religious faith and that she, as a woman, can lead in civilizing the community. These feelings have finally overcome her fears that marriage will subject her to the double standard, demand "only a small part of my brain" (326), and kill love. Probably one reviewer had the ending of this book in mind when jabbing at Sinclair Lewis's *Main Street* (1920): "We should greatly prefer to have our English cousins find in Judith, rather than in Carol Kennicott, the type of the American girl of today."[11]

The conventional ending of the romance plot in marriage has been preserved, but in the course of preservation two subtextual protests against male dominance have been made. One occurs after the Reverend Mr. Fowler says that Judith could help make Lost Chief a great place for children. The wife of the Mormon rancher adds, "If the church didn't hamper her too much. . . . The church and God are both males." The comment is acknowledged by Judith with a "sudden appreciative smile" (346, omissions mine). Thus do both women communicate to readers an awareness that wives and mothers labor under a supernatural patriarchy as well as a terrestrial one.

The other subsurface thrust comes in musings of Douglas that show his increasing sensitivity toward Judith as a person: "What sense of sacrifice, he [Douglas] thought, must a girl like Jude have, in giving up her life to a man?" Even though he sees marriage as possession of woman by man—a possession implied in the phrase "giving up"—he seems also to understand that "Judith would never be any man's really, to know and to hold. . . . 'Forever would he love and she be fair!'" (348–349, omissions mine). Douglas shows more gentleness than roan-breaker John Hardy, and a part of the covert message here is that marriage would be more desirable for women if men understood that companionship rather than male dominance should be a marital goal. Whether the passage is in part ironic is not clear. Did the author wish to imply that, in its original context, the image of courtship suggested by the quotation from Keats's "Ode on a Grecian Urn" includes a stasis and detachment little suited to flesh-and-blood lovers? Whatever the answer, the ending of the novel is not, in the traditional sense, 100 percent "happy."

Judith was a formula Western and much else besides. In *The Exile of the Lariat* (1923), one finds, within the frame of the Western, another inclusion of material from outside that frame, mostly aspects of the political novel as that category is defined by Joseph Blotner.[12] In fact, *Exile* has more of the political novel in it than any other Western this reader has seen, except for a novella, "Shootin'-up Sheriff," discussed in Chapter 7. Other aspects of *Exile* that do not fit into the Western frame include a hero and heroine who at the start of the novel are married but separated and an Other Woman who has successfully pursued a career in finance rather than in a saloon or dance-hall.

The enveloping action is a political campaign in which women frequently move the plot. In a gubernatorial contest set in Wyoming shortly after World War I, women's votes and women's campaign strategy play a large part, although the candidate they serve success-fully is a man (the first woman governor of any state, Nellie Tayloe [sic] Ross, would not take office in Cheyenne until 1925, two years after publication of Morrow's book). The Lariat, a bookshop, func-tions literally and symbolically as a place of exile from the present in the past; in the shop the "exile," Hugh Stewart, a paleontologist, dis-plays his newly discovered fossil treasures. When the place becomes a campaign headquarters where political activists plan electoral strat-egy, it also symbolically gives the present priority over the past. Thus it is associated with the conversion of Hugh Stewart from ivory-tower (or fossil-cave) research to political action and the compromise he eventually makes between the two career opportunities.

His conversion and compromise are motivated largely by two women, his estranged wife Jessie and Miriam Page, who was an "in-vestment advisor" for an Eastern bank until she met Hugh. Although Hugh makes the ultimate decision about his career, both women help move the plot, and although Miriam conventionally loses to the wife in the battle for Hugh's affections, she moves the plot more, perhaps, than either Jessie or Hugh.

In fact, the author wavers between upholding patriarchy, with its repressive ideal of femininity, and supporting the ideals of free-dom and personhood for women—including commitment, if they choose, to full participation in political contests. In one example of authorial indecision, Morrow gives the hero the potential for meta-morphosis into a comic character but does not allow that metamor-phosis to occur. Hugh is presented as "straight" rather than comic when he says to Jessie's mother, "I warn you that I shall show no quarter to family or to any other human being who is trying to block me or manipulate me!" (107). This pomposity is mitigated by nei-ther humor nor irony, although surely few heroes in either Western or domestic fiction have been blocked or manipulated as effectively as Hugh is by Jessie, her mother, Miriam Page, and Mrs. Ellis, his campaign manager.

Jessie and her mother agree that Hugh's talent is political rather than paleontological; indeed, their disagreement with Hugh about his career has been the main cause of his and Jessie's estrangement. Despite—or because of—Hugh's demonstrated accomplishments in the finding and analysis of fossils, Jessie's mother feels he's "wasting his life being a coroner on a lot of beasts that died the Lord knows when" (38). This mother-in-law, both here and later, is comic in her ignorance and narrowness, but she and Jessie get their way. The result is good for Hugh, in spite of himself, and for the people of the state, especially the women and children.

Moreover, the Other Woman adds her manipulative skills to those of Jessie and her mother; in fact, without her influence, the two "good" women might have failed to make an activist of Hugh. Nonetheless, the wife wins him back, and the Other Woman loses him. This outcome is foreshadowed the first time each character is depicted for the reader's eye. In the first sentence of the following description, the author practically labels Jessie as heroine, then typecasts her:

> She was what one likes the western type of woman to be.
> Tall and strong, with fine shoulders and slim thighs.
> Strength in the splendid neck and strength rather than
> beauty in the cleanly chiseled face. Perhaps in her perfect
> strength there was beauty. Who can say? At least her eyes
> were beautiful—eyes, blue, violet, gray, black; eyes with
> shadows in the corners, with humor in the lifting lids,
> with courage and daring in the direct and heart-search-
> ing force of her listening gaze. . . . Yet it was the strength
> of Jessie that remained with you rather than her points of
> beauty (37–38, omissions mine).

The emphasis on strength rather than on beauty suggests that Jessie is more of an Ideal Real Woman than a True Woman—and so, except in one episode, it turns out.

Somewhat similar to yet contrasting with this image is that of Miriam: "She was tall and slender and the most perfectly groomed woman that Hugh had ever seen. From the shining waves of her brown hair, to the shining vamps of her tanned shoes, she was flawless. Her delicate skin was without blemish. So were the lines of her regular, clean-cut features. Her eyebrows arched in two fine curves. . . . [H]er lips parted over the whitest teeth he had ever seen" (62, omissions mine). To some extent Miriam Page resembles Florence Grace Hallman, the female land agent in B. M. Bower's *The Flying U's Last Stand*, who "looked the successful businesswoman to her fingertips" (9). Each exemplifies the career-oriented New Woman, with the mannishness of that stereotype altered by a sex appeal artificially created, and a bit sinister. In the description of Miriam, "shining vamps" and "whitest teeth" bring to mind Lamia, in classical myth a man-devouring monster disguised as a beautiful woman. The threatening aspects of Miriam's image hint accurately that she will eventually lose to the "good" woman in the battle for Hugh's affections. Actually, far from being a monster in disguise, Miriam is "naturally an impulsive human being. But her business training had refined the impulsiveness to a capacity for making instant decisions of a far-seeing kind" (65). One needs to ask, why "but" instead of "and"? In a man this training and capacity would of course be admirable; the author's endowing even an Other Woman with such ability sends one more covert telegram negating the masculine image of woman as mentally inferior.

The author goes on: "She [Miriam] wanted Hugh. She proposed to have him" (65)—for his own good, of course. "He was to belong to her and to that larger world to which his talents and her personality entitled him" (83). These had been exactly Jessie's feelings about Hugh; moreover, Miriam's efforts make the difference in getting Hugh into politics. The Other Woman's decision to politicize Hugh makes her at this point the chief plot-mover, and her moving ultimately turns out well for all concerned—except for Miriam herself. About her, the author veers again toward supporting the conventional image of femininity and seems to sympathize with the characters who want to get rid of her. Ironically, once Miriam has helped push Hugh into the race for governorship, her presence in his life, despite their mutual sexual restraint, would hurt him politically, especially with women voters. His campaign manager, a woman, tells him, "You will have to end the gossip about Miriam Page, and return to your wife" (189).

The author's ambiguous feelings about ideal femininity and

ideal masculinity further complicate the breakup of Hugh and Miriam and the eventual reconciliation of Hugh and Jessie. Jessie, even though married to this man, is unladylike according to the conventions of popular fiction when she offers herself by saying: "Hughie, if Miriam Page were out of the way, I could make you care for me as much as ever" (182). Hugh's reply: "I love Miriam as I could never love a woman again" (182). The "strength" emphasized in the description of Jessie quoted earlier suddenly vanishes, and she reacts more like the ultrafeminine stereotype of the True Woman than like the Ideal Real Woman favored in Morrow's other Westerns: "She wept on and on as if by tears she sought to wash out the mistakes of her selfish girlhood" (183). A true Western hero of the flintier sort, Hugh remains unmoved by this display, but he finally consents to run for the governorship—mainly in order to block the approval of a dam that would destroy a promising fossil site.

However, when he learns that Miriam (moving the plot crucially) has encouraged the prospective dam builders, knowing that their intent to build would furnish the decisive motivation for Hugh's entry into politics, he overreacts with the rhetoric of a man who feels he has idealized the wrong woman. "Miriam, who understood him as no other human being did. Miriam, who was worth sacrificing Jessie for. . . . God in heaven, there was no such Miriam!" (246, omissions mine). The election has not yet been held but Miriam tells Hugh, with only slight exaggeration as things turn out, that, "I've made you governor of Wyoming . . . I've given you to the world," to which Hugh says, "You were crooked with me, Miriam!" (258). Like Jessie, Miriam loses control of her feelings, but she reacts more like a cavewoman—or a stereotyped fancy woman—than like a True Woman: "The ultra-sophistication dropped from her like a cloak and it was the primal woman who hurled herself against Hugh, beating at his chest with her fists. 'Mine!' she screamed. 'No other woman's. Mine!' " (259).

A strong indication that the author's feelings about feminine and masculine roles were mixed is that the reader's feelings remain uncertain. Convention in popular fiction sanctioned manipulation of hero by heroine, provided the woman's goal was to spur the hero toward rehabilitation or achievement. (In one of Helen Hunt Jackson's early domestic tales, the narrator says, "If Jane Miller had been a strong, determined woman, Reuben would not have been a failure. . . . The right sort of wife would have given him both [purpose and courage].) [13] In Hugh's case, the Other Woman promotes his career effectively; she has indeed gone behind his back, but so, later, does Jessie—and Hugh praises her "generosity" (287).

After her outburst of "primal" behavior, Miriam plays the gracious loser by quietly slipping out of Hugh's life—itself an action beneficial to his campaign. This is also a self-sacrifice typical of Other Women with hearts of gold rather than of Lamia figures. Shortly thereafter, Miriam dies of pneumonia. Finding no hints in the text about fate, morality, or retribution, I can only speculate that the author simply wanted to get the love triangle out of the narrative in order to focus on the political progress of Hugh Stewart and his women campaigners. One can hardly help noting that Miriam's pushing of Hugh into politics in the first place gives Jessie the chance not only to work for his election but to offer him, at last, "the thing that makes a man fight to live up to his dreams—the real love of a real woman" (1). Miriam could have given him exactly that.

As for Hugh, the dominant image he presents is that of a hero somewhat confused but essentially "manly"—i.e., patriarchally oriented. He is an achiever handicapped by a wife who does not believe in his work and who "chose to take me not as I was but as something you thought you could make of me" (55). In turning from paleontology to politics, he does not so much yield "unmanfully" to the women as decide to fight for his fossils against the dam builders, and though tricked by a designing female, he has the (manly) character to recover and to go on fighting the good fight. The underlying image on this palimpsest is less complimentary. Hugh is a self-absorbed careerist who, having left his wife, is like the well-known ship without a rudder. He makes avowals of love to a different woman who really does love him (though her love may be overly possessive), but he reacts to her well-intentioned manipulation with a disillusionment that in its unwarranted intensity suggests an unconscious desire to break with her. He regains his self-control in suspiciously short order, returns to his wife for reasons of political expediency, and stays with her only because death has taken the Other Woman.

His compromise between two careers has been made possible in part because of his victimization of the two women in his domestic life. The interpretations are mutually consistent and equally credible, and this equal credibility is itself part of the underlying message. Intentionally or otherwise, the author implies that, hero though he may be, Hugh is also a self-righteous, self-absorbed cad and that the choice of designation depends on whether or not a reader's point of view is patriarchally oriented.

Eventually husband and wife become reconciled in a happy ending that includes Jessie's pledge to help Hugh, after one term in office, to "go back to your dinosaurs" (335). She will step down from the role of First Lady to that of homemaker, once again, for a paleontologist. The conventional ideal of marriage has been formally upheld yet simultaneously subverted—for instance, when Jessie's mother comments, "If only the people who loved each other stayed married, about one marriage in a hundred would survive. . . . Pink [her husband] and I don't care a straw about each other! We stay together simply because I think it's right" (107). Unstated message: Women like Jessie's mother who endure loveless marriages have confused rightness with respectability. The volume of this message remains low because the speaker and her husband seem to get along comfortably despite their lack of mutual affection. Incidentally—maybe not so incidentally—the year (1923) *Exile* was published was also the year following the author's divorce and the year she remarried.

In 1918, when suffragettes picketed the White House in Washington, Morrow as editor and journalist had written that their aim was "noble" but that the tactic they chose was "mean and unpatriotic."[14] In 1923, with the war receding into the past, Morrow the novelist's support of women's political activism was straightforward, at least by comparison with her ambiguous attitude toward individual man-woman relationships. In *Exile* she implied not only that women are in politics to stay but also that whenever political developments affect women, home, and children, political action—and this necessarily means political interaction with men—is a natural extension of women's role as maintainers of home and family as well as an exercise of their rights as citizens. Moreover, men must accept the activism of women. Hugh says that he can't stand the "idea of de-

98   Honoré Willsie Morrow

pending on a lot of women to help me out in what is a real man's fight" (142). Mrs. Ellis, his campaign manager and the most sympathetic character of either gender in the book, "educates" Hugh in part by recounting how, as a girl of twelve, she watched her mother die in childbirth on the family's isolated ranch. She explains how legislation proposed by women would bring medical care within comparatively easy reach of the state's far-flung hamlets and ranches, emphasizing that this legislation can be enacted only with support from some of the men who also favor the dam builders (and therefore destruction of the fossil field). Mrs. Ellis convinces Hugh that the so-called women's issues and the so-called men's fight are interrelated and that the day is past in politics when women can stay home and let men do their fighting for them.

For present-day rediscoverers of *Exile*, mention of birth control, child care, and divorce, let alone discussion of these possibilities, is conspicuous by its absence. Margaret Sanger and Charlotte Perkins Gilman were only two of a number of women activists who had made these alleviations of the married woman's lot known to a considerable public. However, Morrow was among those spokeswomen who worried about "Anglo-Americans" committing "race suicide" through having fewer children per unit of population than "South Europeans."

Having made the deal that, by drawing the support of the women's groups and the dam-related interests, gets him the governorship, Hugh as governor even presses the button that sets off the explosion ruining the fossil site. At that ceremony, a male supporter shouts, "Hughie Stewart is a man!" (356). In context, this implies that manhood includes realization that encouraging women to concentrate on their "racial task" (286) of childbearing has priority over digging up the past, a traditional view.[15] A more general and somewhat less conventional implication of Hugh's deal is that, politically speaking, pregnancy and other family problems are as much men's concerns as women's and that men and women can and should work together on these problems as companions and equals. Further, women do not compromise their femininity by working with men.

The author implies that on the whole men are slow learners of these lessons. Jessie's own father, a former rancher, hangs the nickname "Gray Stallion" on Hugh, implying that a major motive of both the candidate and his "herd" of women supporters is sexual. A Mormon patriarch who eventually supports Hugh and the women confesses, "I'm not used to conferring with women around," and when that conference is recessed, he bolts "like a boy freed from school" (270). For another male supporter of Hugh, a woman he is supposed to "take orders from" represents a trend toward "that perky, smarty, new kind of woman!"[16] Another male conjoins two macho myths in saying about Mrs. Ellis: "She's a woman, ain't she? So no matter how hard she is, she's soft. The same way with professors. I don't want 'em in office" (204).

The women themselves learn quickly to interact politically with each other. "I won't take orders from a woman" (193), says Jessie's mother when asked to work under Mrs. Ellis, but she sheds this male-oriented prejudice and becomes the campaign manager's "right hand" (204). In general, Morrow's depiction of a political sisterhood effectively undermines the traditional view that women should leave politics to the men. The ending, with its patched-up marriage and hints of eventual movement of the heroine toward domestic immurement, seems little more than a token gesture toward that view.

Morrow's work has been left out of two recent collections of writings about the West by women,[17] but it deserves attention beyond the present introductory essay. Like the other authors in this study, Morrow was a frontierswoman of popular letters who tried formula Westerns despite feminist leanings and who made compromises between these leanings and the sexist restrictions of the formula. Her Western fiction raises the questions of why she chose the formula-Western genre and to what degree she sacrificed her ideals about women's rights and personhood in order to publish in that genre. The first question may be plausibly answered by the compound proposition that she was inspired by the West and by her experiences there and that by the time she began to write, the formula Western romance had become so firmly established that there seemed no other path to follow in writing mass-market fiction about that area. The second question invites two possible, if only partial, answers. First, Morrow was by no means a full-fledged feminist. Her inclinations in that direction were weakened in part by her respect for the patriarchally based ideals of her New England ancestors. This respect comes through especially in her nonfictional book about Bronson Alcott and in the historical novel *Black Daniel* (1931), about the second wife of Daniel Webster. Second, Morrow pursued a career in journalism and in writing fiction while functioning as a wife and mother. She married twice and raised three children (her last novel, *Demon Daughter* [1939], was inspired by one of them). Morrow's own division of interest in life, between domesticity and career appears to some extent in her novels. Certain comments in Morrow's Westerns—muted because they are made by characters whom one may not necessarily consider to be speaking for the author—refract that division with especial clarity. For example, the heroine of *Still Jim*, trapped in a bad marriage, omits mention of love in saying that marriage is a duty because it perpetuates "the race" (186). Judith Spencer feels that marriage rarely has much to do with love, and Jessie Stewart's parents remain together because Mrs. Stewart feels that marital permanence is "right"—though no definition is offered for that term. These and other implicit criticisms of marriage as an institution, in combination with the already noted modifications in this author's romance plots, amount to an undermining of the popular ideal on which closure of most formula Westerns is based: the male-dominated home with the invisible wife-mother-servant. Yet Morrow's own endings support that ideal—overtly.[18]

In her own ways, then, Morrow made essentially the same compromise with the Western formula and its built-in sexism as did the other women writers of Westerns introduced herein. Though perhaps less warm in her feminist sympathies than Caroline Lockhart or Vingie E. Roe, she broadened the subject matter of the formula to include woman's search for religious faith and her right to participate actively in politics. She also pioneered on another frontier when she became one of the first formula writers of either gender to offer as a happy ending the marriage of a white heroine to a Native American hero.

Upon reading the diary of Narcissa Whitman, wife of Dr. Marcus Whitman, Morrow was reportedly inspired to go beyond the Western formula and to write historical novels. *We Must March* (1925), based on the missionary efforts and tragic death of these pioneers in the Oregon Territory, was the first of such novels. In 1927 one commentator wrote that "Mrs. Morrow speaks of her earlier Western romances with a savage impatience."[19] However, through these romances Morrow made a significant contribution to the formula Western and, in general, to popular fiction by women. Regardless of her views about her Westerns, this author may well be more important as a writer in that genre than as a writer of historical novels. Her reputation needs overhauling accordingly.

PERSONS, PROPERTY, AND POWER: KATHARINE NEWLIN BURT'S WESTERN HEROINES

Katherine Newlin Burt was once cited as the "wife of Struthers Burt, the novelist."[1] By that time (1930), seven of her twenty-three novels had been published. Three were essentially formula Westerns, and the wife of "the novelist" eventually wrote two more such.

Two of Burt's early novels, *Hidden Creek* (1920) and *Snow Blind* (1921), are essentially domestic tales with Western frontier settings rather than formula Westerns. The focus in each is on a relatively passive heroine and the distresses she endures rather than on adventure and fast action. Of Burt's formula Westerns, *The Branding Iron* (1919) and a much later work *The Tall Ladder* (1932), hold the most significance for students of the Western and of popular fiction by women, the first because of its provocative message about women as chattels and the second because of the consistency with which the heroine dominates the story and moves the plot.

Broadly speaking, Burt resembles other women writing in the Western genre. Like them, she regards the formula as a problem rather than as a set of rules and manipulates it by means of the double-voice strategy. She also starts out several (though not all) of her Western heroines young and alone in the world, without responsible family or effectively helpful friends but with the actual or potential attributes of the Ideal Real Woman: a robust physique, a will to independence, a desire for education and the ability to earn a living on their own. The result of Burt's efforts in the Western field is a body of fiction readable from two viewpoints, that of the indiscriminate consumer of mass-market Westerns and that of the reader who discerns and reacts to the criticisms of male domination implied therein.[2] In general, this is the same result obtained by other writers introduced in this volume.

Like Owen Wister, Burt and her husband were Easterners from affluent families. In fact, Maxwell Struthers Burt had known Wister during college days and, as the Burts' son Nathaniel put it later, "wrangled" Wister as one of the "dudes" for the guest ranch he operated near Jackson, Wyoming. According to Nathaniel, on one occasion his mother "not only sat but lay at Wister's feet." Unseated by her mount, she regained her bearings to find Wister "taking notes in his little pocket book on just how a lady looks when thrown from a horse."[3] None of this is to imply that Burt shared Wister's conventional views about women; on the contrary, all of her novels, Western and otherwise, encourage a "strongly feminist viewpoint."[4]

Katharine Newlin was born in 1882 and received most of her education from governesses and at a private school from which, as she wrote later, "I 'graduated' at the age of seventeen and had no further formal education. I was considered 'finished'."[5] At thirty-one she married Burt, and for a while she lived the life of a belated but genuine pioneer wife and mother at the Wyoming ranch. The Burts had a son and a daughter, born in a log cabin during blizzards in 1913 and 1915, respectively. Struthers Burt wrote later that the son came when "I was driving a band of forty horses through the whirling madness to their winter feeding grounds."[6] Much later, Katharine served as fiction editor of the *Ladies' Home Journal* (1928–1930).[7]

As a writer, the husband attracted attention before the wife, and her second volume, *Hidden Creek,* is dedicated to "Maxwell Struthers Burt, who blazed the trail." His first collection of short stories appeared in 1918; two more collections and three novels by him came out within the next ten years.[8] His short story "Each in His Generation" won the O. Henry Memorial Award Prize in 1920. By that year, Katharine had written her first and most provocative novel, *The Branding Iron*; her twenty-third and last novel appeared in 1968. Writing in 1983, Nathaniel Burt commented that "my mother's career, though far less seriously considered [than my father's], has been more durable," noting that all of Struthers Burt's books were out of print, whereas many of Katharine's were "still available."[9]

In *The Diary of a Dude Wrangler*, Struthers Burt referred to "one of the grimmest stories I ever remembered hearing, of a girl who was branded by her father because of some trouble she had with a young man, and of how her father was shot from ambush the next day, and his murderer was never discovered" (293). Katharine drew on this incident in writing her first novel, *The Branding Iron*, serialized in 1919 by *Everybody's Magazine* (which also published Western fiction by Vingie E. Roe and Honoré Willsie Morrow). About one-third of the action of *The Branding Iron* takes place in the East, but the tale is typical of Westerns in that simple, Old West values are contrasted favorably with the superior taste and polish but inferior morals of Easterners. In addition, this novel shows the author's internal conflict between rebellion against the patriarchal view of women as property and the demand of the formula Western that women accept that status. Like other women writers who coped with the Western formula, Burt partially revolved this conflict by using two levels of text to express in toned-down fashion her criticisms of the patriarchy.

In the early twentieth century and throughout the nineteenth, the heroine of much popular fiction was, at the start of the narrative, an Eve type innocent about evil. But in *The Branding Iron*, Joan Carver knows from childhood more about the seamy side of sex than most fictional innocents learn until marriage, if then. Joan has been brought up in isolation by a type common in both the Western and the domestic novel, a defective parent[10]—in this case a "hideous father" who often dumps on her the details of how he discovered his wife was unfaithful and executed her. " 'That was yer mother, gel; she was a bad woman.' There followed a coarse and vivid description of her badness and the manner of it. . . . 'I found her'—again the rude details of his discovery—'I found him, an' I let him go for the white-livered coward he was, but her I killed. I shot her dead. . . . ' " He would then tell Joan how he stole her from an aunt when she was three and took her to his trapper's shack "to do my work an' to look after my comfort." He goes on. "There ain't a-goin' to be no man in *yer* life, Joan" (7–8, original emphasis). Through this early and singular "education" about evil, Joan is invested with an animal-like sensuality and bearing that fundamentally affects her later fortune.

Brand her physically the father does not; the author transfers that action to Joan's husband. At seventeen, Joan runs away and finds work as a waitress. Within a week, mutual love at first sight strikes her and Pierre Landis. Pierre takes her to a magistrate for the marriage ceremony and then to his small ranch. After two weeks, during which "their love, unanalyzed, was as joyous as the loves of animals" (21), Joan's father tracks them down. Within a few minutes he —incredibly—poisons Pierre's mind so effectively with the story of Joan's mother's behavior that, after a local minister has lent Joan some books and thereby aroused Pierre's jealousy, he stamps into her shoulder with a white-hot iron the same "Two-Bar" brand with which he has marked his cattle, his other property. Coincidentally, a stranger approaching the isolated cabin (the season is midwinter) hears Joan's screams, enters, and shoots the menacing torturer. Thinking at first that he has killed Pierre, he prepares to take Joan away.

Unconventionally, this rescuer is the villain; more convention-ally, the apparent villain will turn out to be the hero and the appar-ent hero the villain. Prosper Gael has seen movement by Pierre that indicates he is still alive, but he carries Joan off despite her objec-tions to leaving her husband, even to leaving him, as she thinks, dead. Gael, a writer, takes Joan to a mountain retreat that he had built for the wife of another man, a woman who has not joined him there because, by her own confession, she has "failed in courage" (170). During this retreat sequence, the dominant message of the text is one of sympathy for the rescuer: "Whatever one must think of Prosper Gael, it is difficult to shirk heartache on his account" (62), because in place of the woman who never came he brought Joan "as a lonely man brings in a wounded bird to nurse and cherish" (62–63). The muted message, however, is that to him she is indeed an animal, this message foreshadows what soon follows.

At this point, a comparison of woman with unruly animals ap-pears that is similar to those analogies in B. M. Bower's *Chip* and in

Honoré Willsie Morrow's "Breaking the Blue Roan" and carrying the same twofold message. The dominant one: Woman's destiny is service to man, but she deserves gentleness and understanding from man (what else was new in 1919, or long before?). The underlying communication: More than merely accepting gentleness, women should insist on their right to be partners and friends, not servants or possessions.

Prosper Gael starts writing a novel about how he is taming and educating an "enchanted leopardess." Emotionally exhausted, Joan has trusted Gael "as simply, as singly, as foolishly as a child trusts God" (71). But when Gel finds out that Pierre has indeed survived, he violates that trust by keeping the news to himself; as part of his "education" of Joan he trains her to be his paramour. "The whole duty of woman," he lectures, "is to *charm*" (85, original emphasis). He also "teaches" that "marriage is the sin against the Holy Ghost. . . . [I]t's recommended as the lesser of two evils by a man who despised woman as only an Oriental can despise her, Saint Paul" (140–141, omissions mine). Later he calls marriage "man's most studied insult to woman (254). Although the author reduces Gael's libertinistic arguments to "modern philosophy, tricked out by a ready wit" (102), an undertone is there for those who will listen with the third ear: No less than adultery, marriage, too, is a kind of servitude.

Partly through his arguments, Gael succeeds in seducing and impregnating Joan, and the author subsequently gives the formula a wrench in that Joan is not "ruined" but is headed toward a conventional happy ending. Before he knows that Joan is pregnant, Prosper gets a letter from his former flame pleading for a reconciliation and abruptly leaves for the East, promising of course to return.

Having discovered the letter, Joan abandons the retreat and bears the child sired by Prosper. It does not live, and later, after a series of coincidences—too many even for an early Western—Joan is brought to New York City by a theatrical producer, who finds her a "natural" for the lead part in "The Leopardess," a dramatization by Gael of his novel about "taming" and "civilizing" Joan. In rehearsals, she is disturbed by the haunting familiarity of the situation and conceives a dislike for the author, whose identity has been kept secret for publicity purposes. The play opens and is a hit.

Reenter Pierre. Approximately four years have elapsed since the branding, and an acute sense of guilt has made him feel a new love for Joan and given him greater understanding of himself. Even so, his release from guilt depends on his regaining Joan's love and respect. He goes to the play but does not at first recognize Joan. Eventually Prosper Gael publicly reveals himself as the author, and Joan realizes that he has all along treated her as writer's material—as psychological if not physical property. She attacks him physically on stage, and in the struggle her shoulder is bared; the brand becomes visible, and Pierre recognizes Joan at last. Wife and husband are reconciled, and Prosper waxes sarcastic: "So, after all, the branding iron is the proper instrument. . . . A man can always recognize his estray, and when she is recognized, she will come to heel." But Joan denounces Gael as a coldhearted manipulator of her mind and soul: "The hurts you get from love, they heal. . . . Pierre was mad through loving me, too ignorantly, too jealously, but what you did to me was through loving me too little" (305–307, omissions mine).

To Pierre, Joan insists, "I am bad. I left you for dead and I went away" (309)—though she had been led to believe he really was dead. Pierre counters that the entire guilt is his alone. Joan has been compared not only to a "clean, wild thing," a leopardess, a panther, and a wildcat but also repeatedly to a child. She and Pierre represent the natural savagery and equally natural humanity of the West in contrast to the dehumanizing artificiality of the East. The author's wish to sustain this comparison, perhaps as much as her determination to force the romance plot into a conventional ending with lovers reconciled, accounts for Joan's feeling more guilty at having left the supposedly defunct Pierre than for having borne a child out of wedlock to a faithless lover. The author's mixed motives also account for the barely plausible revival of Joan's love for her one-time torturer. After leaving Prosper's hideaway, Joan had told the drunken husband of an abused wife, "You don't own Mabel. . . . She belongs to her own self" (156, omissions mine). Yet at the end, once Pierre has forgiven her "abandonment" of him and her adultery, she again becomes "his."

Where, then, is the alleged feminist slant of this author? Until and including the ending, the muted messages favor the female viewpoint. Sometimes Joan moves the plot; from time to time she is servant or victim, but she is always the main character, invested with an importance denied any of the male characters. In addition, instead of suffering any of the punishments decreed by tradition for the woman who goes morally astray, Joan rises to stardom in the theater and to a conventionally happy ending. The unspoken message in the author's thus tampering with the romance plot is that under certain circumstances a "fallen" woman may be considered merely naive rather than sinful; therefore she may subsequently mature and even marry respectably. In contrast, Betty Morena, Prosper's former mistress, has through her lack of "courage" guaranteed the continuance of a loveless marriage in which she will be dominated to the point of abuse. The subversive implication is that for some oppressed wives, adultery, with all its drawbacks, might be preferable to the physical and emotional slavery of marriage; let the men beware.

Even after the embrace of the already married lovers in the final scene, the double voicing continues. Presumably, Joan will abruptly terminate a career that epitomizes the pretense and hypocrisy of the East and return with Pierre to the "wild and clean" West—represented by the isolated ranch where Joan will be homemaker. However, the meeting at which she and Pierre become reconciled has itself been arranged as an "experiment" by the doctor attending the distraught Joan, and the last words in the book are given to the doctor's reassurance "as to the success of this experiment" (310). The pleasure of the lovers at their reunion provides the dominating mood of the ending, but present also is the low-key reminder that Joan once again has been manipulated by a man—and aren't women too often treated thus?

On the whole, reviewers of *The Branding Iron* ignored or failed to catch the controversial innuendoes against regarding women as chattels, perhaps because they read the book as light escapist fiction. Typical was the comment in the *Nation* that the work "sustains, of course, no relation to reality."[11] This attitude may or may not have been reflected among mass-market readers or among moviegoers;

the book was reprinted twice within a year and was made the basis for a film but seems to have attracted little attention since.

❦

Among the writers introduced in this volume, Burt excels in evoking Western landscape as a force in the lives and feelings of her characters. Although not a formula Western, *Hidden Creek,* Burt's next novel, includes more depiction of landscape as such a force than any of her formula novels and therefore merits at least a nod. One of the most effective bits of impressionistic landscape in this book occurs after the teenage heroine has been assaulted by her hotel-keeper employer and has fled, alone on a pony, the Rocky Mountain town where she was abused:

> Her sudden loneliness descended upon her with an almost audible rush. Dusk at this height—dusk with a keen smell of glaciers and wind-stung pines—dusk with the world nine thousand feet below; and about her this falling-away of mountain-side, where the trees seemed to slant and the very flowers to be outrun by a mysterious sort of flight of rebel earth toward space! The great and heady height was informed with a presence which if not hostile was terrifyingly ignorant of man. There was some one not far away, she felt, just above there behind the rocky ridge, just back there in the confusion of purplish darkness streaked by pine-tree columns, just below in the thicket of the stream—some one to meet whose look meant death (174).

The re-creation of a mountain setting by this tenderfoot's overactive imagination drives her into dependence on a deranged female recluse in male clothing and on a hero type who before the end proves unheroic and unreliable. "Real" nature—blizzards and sub-zero weather—reinforce Sheila's dependency but eventually play a part in her release from these people. Though the focus is always on the heroine and her interpersonal relationships, the author uses

Western weather and topography not as a backdrop but literally as part of the foreground of action.

〜〜〜〜

The heroine of *The Tall Ladder* is no teenaged waif but a divorcee of twenty-eight whose will and independent ways suggest the male-female dissonance within the author, who by this time had established herself both as a writer of popular fiction (this novel was her ninth) and as a ranch wife and a mother. The conflict between Burt's feminist inclinations and her desire to work within the Western formula also shows in her depiction of the female protagonist's adventures in the West and her role in a romance plot, the ending of which is happy in a sense but, from the patriarchal viewpoint, flawed.

Julia Oliphant has an independent fortune and an "unfeminine" will, both inherited from her father. Like him, "She was Hannibal, she was Napoleon. . . ." (53, omissions mine). As the narrative begins she has divorced her husband, who is serving a prison sentence for his part in a stock-market swindle; his guilt lay chiefly in trusting the wrong people, including Locksley Greene, to whom Julia has become engaged after the divorce. Jasper Clere, the ex-husband, is released from prison, and the guilt-ridden Julia breaks her engagement and flees to the West. Beginning with this action, she functions as the chief mover of the plot. On a whim she buys a ranch in the northern Rockies. Feeling like an outlaw for breaking her Eastern ties, she deceives the local lawmen and saves from capture a fugitive, Jeff Wager, who is wanted for a crime he hasn't committed (Julia doesn't even know yet what he's wanted for). According to Diana Reep, in popular fiction the "unnatural" rescue of a man by a woman usually has negative results for the woman. Even if the two are potential mates, the woman, Reep says, is seldom rewarded with the love of the man.[12] Burt changes this aspect of the formula only slightly: After Julia has hired Jeff as foreman for the ranch he does fall in love with her, but eventually he rejects her just as she is steeling herself to reject him.

Among other accomplishments, Jasper is an experienced horse trainer. Guilt about having divorced him during his prison term motivates Julia to lure him West with the promise of work on the ranch. Before he knows the identity of his new boss, Jasper taunts Jeff about working for a woman; they fight but afterward become friends. An implied message of the fight and of the subsequent male bonding is that the gender of one's employer should be of no concern to employees or anybody else. But when Jasper finds out that his employer is his ex-wife, he tries to quit. Julia gets Jeff to drag him back at the end of a lasso, and he then decides to stay on, thereby showing that his will is less strong than hers.

A subplot features another strong-willed woman, Ma Orme, whom Julia hires as cook and housekeeper. She too moves the plot, and not too gently. Her son, a wanted criminal, is hiding near the ranch, and Ma Orme, having already knocked out Jeff with brass knuckles because she thinks he's killed a man her son has actually killed, treats the sheriff likewise when he comes for Jeff. She even contrives the escape of her son in the car carrying the injured lawman. She too has rescued a man she loves, but she goes unrewarded. Meanwhile, the formula rule that crime must be punished remains unbroken: A few miles down the road her son loses control of the escape car and is killed in the resulting crash. Even so, through the domination of the subplot by this strong female character the idea is put across that Western mothers were not necessarily passive and decorous "sunbonnet saints."

As with Ma Orme, part of the significance of Julia's character and actions is that a strong will in a woman is in itself admirable. However, like Lockhart's Kate Prentice and Roe's Belle Dawson, Julia also demonstrates that the stronger the will, the greater the need for understanding of oneself and for empathy with others. From her Western experiences Julia learns a good deal about others, specifically about certain men. She comes to understand that Greene, the Easterner, is "infinitely more primitive, more sentimental" (217)—that is, more sexist—than Jeff, the Western, and she has matured enough to recognize the strength of the latter's will and to accept his rejection of her.

What Julia learns about herself is less clear. In breaking with her, Jeff says, "We're made out of the same hot, hard, iron stuff. Your will and mine. It [their married life] would be a terrible long, cruel fight" (177–178). Implication: Whatever their gender, persons who value their independence should be especially cautious about marital commitment. In American society circa 1930 as well as in the traditional romance plot, the male was expected to dominate the marital alliance; therefore the unstated message of the breakup includes an especial warning for women that for them the alliance usually meant lifelong domestic servitude.

Julia will never be dominated; on the contrary, she shows signs of continuing her dominating ways. Jasper decides to return to the East and clear his name "alone," but she urges that they remarry and that she share his struggle, as much for her own sake as for his. "It would crucify me with humiliation and with despair if you . . . chose to go back alone." To herself but not to Jasper she says, "If I am his wife I can help him, I can pay off his obligation. . . . I have so much money . . . more than enough to clear his name. We shall be living here [at the ranch]. . . . There will always be enough to run Flying O" (255, omissions mine).

They will remarry, but in the reunion are encoded two mutually dissonant sets of messages. In one set: divorce is regrettable but remarriage of a divorced pair is a satisfactory atonement for both parties. However, trouble still lies in wait for this strong-minded woman and for the two men with whom she has been involved. The prediction is insinuated through two aspects of the reunification. First, from the point of view of most accredited heroes of Westerns (and of their sympathizing readers), this heroine has made two unacceptable choices: deciding that their permanent home will be the ranch without consulting her mate, and using her fortune in restoring a reputation that, according to the code of the formula Western, should be rebuilt by the man's efforts alone. Even readers of the time whose sympathies were with the woman rather than with the man could surely see that Julia's willpower still exceeded her empathy with Jasper as well as her knowledge of the code.

The other set of messages? Jeff Wager, who has qualified as a Western hero at least as much as Jasper, does not, at the end, ride into the sunset; instead he half-promises to return to the ranch as an employee of the woman he had until recently hoped would be his wife. One implication of both these developments is that future conflict in the marriage of Julia and Jasper is likely; another, more encouraging to readers distrustful of the patriarchy, is that whatever her misjudgments and whatever form her future marital trouble may take, Julia is not the sort of woman to sink into invisibility. Burt has followed the romance-plot pattern to a traditional end in wedlock—in this case, in remarriage—but she has also sowed the seeds of destruction of this union. Roe did essentially the same for the strong-willed heroines of *Black Belle* and *The Golden Tide*.

Emotional and practical betterment come to Burt's Western heroines more from their own efforts than through help from the heroes, an imbalance common in domestic novels and fairly frequent in Westerns by women but uncommon in Westerns by men. Burt further warps the formula frame by making the heroine instead of the hero the protagonist—a displacement that occurs in three of her five Westerns—thereby implying that women deserve as much interest and respect as do men. This idea also pervades two of the three Burt Westerns in which the heroine dominates the story even though she is not the protagonist: *A Man's Own Country* and *Men of Moon Mountain*. In these two novels and in *This Woman and This Man,* Burt also modifies the standard romance-plot ending to allow the newly married heroine an unusual degree of freedom, hinting that such freedom might undermine male hegemony in the new household. *A Man's Own Country* closes with the heroine making decisions about ranching and the hero agreeing ironically: " 'Tis your country, lady,' he said, 'and I'm your man. I hev stopped fightin'.' "(261). *This Woman* ends with the woman managing the ranch while her husband practices law, and *Moon Mountain* closes with the hero shaken and dependent on a heroine who has become his mother surrogate as well as his wife. In each of these endings, convention is served formally, but independence for married women is encouraged substantially.

Burt is a radical neither in ideology nor in the practice of writing Western fiction. Nonetheless she created heroines who, as a group, dominated the novels in which they appeared and surpassed the ostensible heroes in resolution and independence of mind. In making these heroines, Burt surely owed much to the domestic novel. In any case, though less bound by the Western formula than

B. M. Bower, less satirical than Caroline Lockhart, less melodramatic than Vingie E. Roe, and less interested in history and religion than Honoré Willsie Morrow, Burt, like them, used the strategy of the double voice to cope with the restrictions of the formula Western and to depict a fictional West in the process of becoming a woman's country a well as a man's.

OTHER AUTHORS

In addition to the material surveyed in previous chapters, contributions to the formula Western were made by other largely forgotten women writers. At least five such deserve more than mere citation. Marah Ellis Ryan brought up some of the problems arising from the attraction of Caucasian men to Native American women; Forrestine Cooper Hooker put two heroes and two heroines into a single extended-family relationship; Cherry Wilson spun a fantasy about women taking over the government of a raw border town; and late in the development of the formula Western, two women writing as "Lillian Janet" produced historical novels about the difficulties encountered and surmounted by women in gold-rush California and post-silver-rush Nevada. Like most of the other writers introduced in this study, these five made women the dominant characters in their versions of the mythic West. They also employed the double-voiced discourse, notably in either modifying or omitting the romance plot.

After the death of her Native American husband, the half-blood (tribe unspecified) title character of Helen Hunt Jackson's best-selling *Ramona* (1884) marries her Latino foster-brother, and both are allowed by the author to live. In two lesser-known novels of the 1890s, Marah Ellis Ryan also showed how the problems of a woman of an ethnic minority might reflect in aggravated form the problems of oppressed women in upper- and middle-class white society. In *The Bondwoman* (1899)—not a Western but a historical romance of the Civil War—a French marquise turns out to be the daughter of an octoroon and still legally the slave of a Southern master. At one point she ponders, "Was it true that certain slavish natures in women—whether of Caucasian or African blood—loved best the men who were tyrants? Was it a relic of inherited tendencies when all women of whatever complexion were but slaves to their masters—called husbands?" (387–388).

Seven years earlier, in *Squaw Élouise* (1892), Ryan had raised similar questions. Élouise is only one-fourth Indian but has been reared as a member of a Pacific Northwest tribe in which women may be held as slaves, as is this eighteen-year-old heroine. Recently purchased by Neil Dunbar, a white trapper from the East, Élouise has fallen in love with her owner. Dunbar exemplifies inconsistencies in white men's notions of honor; he lets his chattel preserve her virginity, but while drunk he gambles her away to another white man. Élouise stabs Dunbar, wounding him severely, then tries to stab herself. He prevents her attempted suicide and, regretting his bargain, helps her to escape from her new owner. She guides Dunbar to a remote forest cave wherein he lies delirious for many days; she nurses him devotedly and almost surely saves his life. He does not know it was she who had knifed him and feels guilty about having put her body up as a wager; she feels guilty about the stabbing. After partially recovering from his wound, he offers her an idyllic (from his point of view) life with him in the mountains and is indignant at the curtness of her refusal.

> If she had reproached him, as he felt it was perfectly reasonable to expect; had complained in woman fashion, and in the same fashion let herself be coaxed into forgiving and forgetting; if she had done like that, as would have done the greater part of the women he knew; then he would have understood just how to manage her. She would have sobbed away her moody anger and been petted into smiles again, and the miserable days of hiding would have become less dreary by her presence. But if

she was going to stand on her dignity and an Indian
grudge in that fashion. . . . (84).

One implication here is that although women of this tribe may cus-
tomarily submit to enslavement, their feelings do not flow in the
grooves of response expected by the white patriarchy; therefore
these tribeswomen cannot be manipulated by white males as easily as
can white women.

Through careful nursing but also through prevarication about
how much he still needs rest, Élouise holds Dunbar, one might say, a
prisoner of love, but her motives are confused and contradictory.
She is "self-ostracized from her gods, fearful of the hell of the Chris-
tians, yet stubbornly facing the prospect of it for the sake of her
human god." Here is an innuendo critical of Christian fundamental-
ism as well as of Christian patriarchalism. Élouise scarcely realizes
"the meaning of the sentiment that had made her turn fierce and
devoted, proud and then slave-like" (109). On one level she is the
stereotyped barbarian maiden who has lost her heart to a white man;
for those who read below the surface, the clear message is that
Élouise is trying to assert her independence as a woman even as she
submits to the demand of both white and Native American cultures
for the female's total subservience to the male she loves. In addition,
from day to day she fears that "some chance would reveal that he was
free to walk away if he chose" (117). The covert message: Under the
double standard in white society husbands are relatively free to walk
away, and many wives have virtually enslaved themselves to hold their
mates, sometimes without being aware of their self-enslavement or
realizing that by accepting the double standard they are in essence
creating their own captivity, forging their own chains.

Dunbar's feelings also show confusion. To him Élouise is a
"guardian angel" and thus cannot be approached sexually. He grows
restless in the custody of a woman "whom he might have loved if he
had not seen in her merely a slave who was devoted. It is not devo-
tion men love, but change" (148). Implication: Men demand variety
and spunk in their female slaves, and the demand is inconsistent
with women's slavery. When a half–Native American missionary
priest offers to marry the pair, Dunbar says, "Élouise can choose her

own life, as other women have done. If she chooses to remain with me, she will not be sorry." but he will not marry a "squaw." To this racism and to the typical overestimation by a man of women's freedom, he adds, "White men owe a duty to their own race when they pick their wives, and their race does not approve of Indians in their families" (217). His attempt to justify his racism on grounds of duty and then by acknowledgment of social pressure without noting the inconsistency reveals his own unthinking slavery to white mores. The priest, Élouise's one-time tutor, nearly strangles Dunbar with his bare hands and desists only when Élouise puts a knife-point to her own throat and threatens, "You will kill us both!" (220). Thus, for the second time she has saved Dunbar's life—and moved the plot.

This unheroic hero's conscience goes on giving him trouble about Élouise: "She had called him 'master' and had served him as a slave; but . . . he felt that she had risen above him, beyond him." When she tells him, "It was revenge made me guard you. . . . Indian revenge—but it is done, and my heart is tired. Go!" Dunbar vacillates. "You shall go too," he begins, and he calls her "*opitsah*" (sweetheart), but she replies bitterly, "No more *opitsah!*" Squaw Élouise, slave Élouise, only" (228, omissions mine). Only not quite: in setting him free, she in a sense becomes the master and he the slave, especially as she also "gives" him to the woman who has adored him since she was fifteen "and whose white face is there on that chain of your throat [in a locket]" (228).

Élouise dies from the bite of a rattlesnake whose mate Dunbar had killed. Her sacrifice is symbolic, but her death is literal, and the manner of it indicates a contrivance the purpose of which is simply to make the ending of this romance plot a conventional one. Diana Reep has shown that when a Native American girl rescued a white man in popular romances, the social taboo against miscegenation caused most writers to turn to "death for the Indian maiden."[1] The two-voice strategy may here operate in reverse. The book's message about what male chauvinism, Indian and white, does to women was socially unpalatable, yet it may have outweighed the conventional but barely brushed-in message at closure that the ideal marriage is that of a white hero to a passive and virginal white woman young enough to look up to him as a father figure and quasi-god as well as a husband. This kind of ending is proper regardless of the hero's previous conduct concerning any sexually attractive but socially ineligible female.

~~~~~

Forrestine Cooper Hooker, daughter and sister of U.S. Army officers, niece of a naval officer, and wife of an "Arizona cattle baron's son,"[2] wrote two novels with Southwestern desert settings. For our purposes the more significant of the two works is *The Long, Dim Trail* (1920). Published by Alfred A. Knopf in a series entitled "Western Stories," this work, despite the inclusion of considerable violence, may be classed as a domestic Western.

Trail includes two plots, somewhat awkwardly brought together in the novel. The first plot incorporates two modifications of the Western formula. One: The woman with whom Allan Traynor, a desert rancher, falls in love is a widow with a child. Two: The wedding occurs less than one-third of the way through the book. Afterward, the episodes featuring the Traynors are distinctly family matters; indeed, before the wedding the hired personnel on Traynor's Diamond H ranch have already become part of an extended family, much like the people on B. M. Bower's Flying U and Mary K. Maule's X Bar B. Limber, Holy, Bronc, and Roarer are hardworking, fun-loving bachelor punchers who welcome the new wife and son with a hilariously bungled attempt to repaper and whitewash the interior of the ranch house. They also offer riding lessons for the boy. Small wonder that "the life on the ranch was like a series of fairy tales to Nell and the boy Jamie in these first days of their home-coming" (131). Subsequently, however, most of the episodes concerning this family circle develop from an illness that Jamie barely survives and from a drought. The four cowboys demonstrate their familial feeling by working merely for room and board, without pay, to help the Traynors survive financially.

The second plot of Hooker's novel arises from the distresses of its protagonist, Katherine Glendon, who fights for personal and family life on another, smaller desert ranch. Relevant to her situation is the statement by Annette Kolodny in *The Land Before Her*: "[T]he

Adams and Eves of the domestic fictionists appear anomalous. Their figures are no longer familiar to us, and—except in the degraded version of the cowboy reluctantly tamed and married by a civilizing schoolmarm—their story seems to have left no lasting imprint on our shared cultural imagination."[3] Kolodny's exception is significant. Degraded or not, the formula-Western version of the new Adam and Eve did indeed make a lasting imprint on our cultural imagination—in fiction by men. In formula Westerns by women, the new Eve often struggles with problems that turn her into something different—for example, the Britomart type presented by Vingie Eve Roe, the self-reliant scuffler of Caroline Lockhart's fiction, or the reluctant martyr type, of which Honoré Willsie Morrow's Penelope Dennis in *Still Jim* and Katherine Glendon in *The Long, Dim Trail* are specimens.

For eight years Katherine Glendon has tried to build a nuclear family circle—on a ranch appropriately named the Circle Cross—despite opposition from an environment that includes "a sky as hard and defiant as the mountains that stared back at it: a masculine sky—a masculine country" (40). She must also contend with an alcoholic husband whose neglect of wife and child is replaced by physical abuse after he realizes that the nearest medical man, Dr. Cuthbert Powell, harbors a chaste and chivalrous love for Katherine. This desert knight behaves as a hero whose profession is healing should. When assaulted by Glendon and a crony, he subdues them effectively but painlessly with his bare hands. Later Glendon attacks the doctor with his fists, but Powell firms up his hero credentials by beating him again in this way of fighting. He finally cows Glendon into signing a written confession of his cattle-rustling, then uses that paper to prevent Glendon from sending his and Katherine's son, now seven, away to a grandfather who would teach him that "all women are inferior in intellect and reason, weak in moral force, and must be treated accordingly" (202). As Powell points out, "A woman has no legal right to her child in Arizona, but neither has a father if he is a convict" (222). Muted but clear is the message that at least at the time of this story (1886 or a bit earlier), women had equal rights—with convicts.

Glendon is both the defective father of the domestic novel and a stereotyped villain of the Western; he rustles, has committed one murder, and will kill again. However, Hooker puts more emphasis on the character and plight of Katherine. In her efficiency, courage, resourcefulness, and protectiveness as a mother, this reluctant martyr is also an Ideal Real Woman. In her fidelity to her abusive husband she is not. A perfect example of this type would separate herself and the child from the oppressive spouse and parent, although, as Frances B. Cogan has noted, "Divorce was unthinkable."[4] As a nearly Ideal Real Woman, Katherine embodies a dual message, illustrated when, twenty-four hours after an Apache raid on the Circle Cross, she serves an unexpected caller, Dr. Powell, a "genteel" luncheon—tasty food on a clean tablecloth. When the doctor compares her favorably to "some of my hysterical woman patients" she replies, "Women living on ranches learn to adapt themselves to many things that would seem hardships to other women" (59). In this reply, by deflecting any implied criticism of her inexcusably absent husband, she exemplifies the ideal loyal helpmate but also transmits a covert message that desert ranch life may encourage matriarchal independence.

In Katherine, this independence is associated with frankness; she makes no pretense of love to Glendon but tells him she has "struggled to keep you from sinking lower, just because you were the father of my boy" (203); note the "my." She is also frank with herself, seeing in retrospect that "what she had mistaken for love, had been reaction against the dull monotony of life with Ann [her sister] and Aunt Jane, and a longing for some outlet for her repressed emotions" (247). She is frank too with Powell, an honorable and therefore all the more insidious tempter. The doctor points out that "Glendon's conviction [for rustling] is sufficient to justify your appeal for a divorce," to which, as an Ideal Real Woman, she counters, "He is my husband. Only death can cancel that obligation." Marriage to Glendon is "my atonement." she adds, "Oh, why does God let us make such terrible mistakes when He knows that we have only one little life to live?" (336–337). Here as in other Westerns by authors of either gender (except Honoré Willsie Morrow's *Judith*), a religious question is asked but then for the moment ignored. However, Katherine does indicate that her fidelity is largely motivated by guilt.

After Glendon breaks jail, she continues to help him until a bolt of lightning strikes him dead. Two possible explanations for this contrivance may be offered. One is the author's intent to convey a dominant message that such victims and villains as Katherine and her husband invite direct remedial action from a divine source. Another possible explanation is more radical and thus necessarily muted: nothing short of action approaching the suddenness and force of nature at its most extreme can change the ways of many men toward women. In this explanation the lightning becomes a metaphor for a woman's revolution. Admittedly, however, the plot contrivance remains arbitrary to the point of outrageousness.

After her husband's death, Katherine slips into an emotional and physical inertia during which she neglects her son completely. Nell Traynor, Allan's wife, eventually helps her to pull out of this inertia, a state apparently induced by guilt at having unconsciously wished for and thereby helped to cause her husband's death. Meanwhile, Dr. Powell and Allan Traynor have merged their holdings and to them have added Katherine's ranch (presumably with her permission). They have then deeded a share in the combined properties to each of the four loyal cowpunchers and begun to build, on part of the land, a sanitarium for crippled children. After Katherine's recovery, the plans for this institution are discussed among Powell, Traynor, Nell and Katherine, and "the two women . . . made many suggestions the men overlooked" (359). In both the economic and social senses this new "ranch" will encompass a happy family further extended to include foster children.

As preparations for the new household progress, Katherine at last feels ready for marriage with Dr. Powell. In this modified happy ending, the author's questioning of the patriarchal order is partially offset by her implicit support of that order. On the one hand, Nell and Katherine have established a sisterhood uncommon in Western fiction since Alfred Henry Lewis's women in Wolfville, and their role as homemakers has expanded to include management of an institutionalized, extended family on a sound economic basis, with several female—and male—employees to ease the workload of the managers. On the other hand, most of the women's suggestions concern "toys, games, books with wonderful fairy-tales" (359); men are still the breadwinners, and the two women are, after all, still primarily homemakers.

Yet a reader may well be induced by the two-level text to vacillate in interpreting the ending of this book. Ryan in *The Bondwoman* had asked her question about women's slavishness and men's mastery twenty-one years earlier. Whether or not Hooker read Ryan's novel, she extends the question to include whether women should also consider themselves slaves to a divinity whose tyranny they may well have overestimated. As Dr. Powell points out to Katherine, in feeling that "only death" can end her duty to her husband, she is ignoring her duty to the child he would oppress. This overt argument by the doctor also includes the covert message that God does not demand the unconditional obedience of wives to husbands that He demands for Himself from His children; men should not be obeyed like gods by their wives, Christian tradition to the contrary notwithstanding. Thus, the religious question Katherine briefly raises is not totally ignored after all.

On the positive side, from a present-day point of view, Katherine has progressed from submissive, oppressed wife to comrade and lover in a context that encourages interaction between men and women for common goals beyond maintaining the nuclear family. Hooker shares with Bower an interest in the extended ranch family, and Hooker's alternative to nuclear homemaking prefigures the temporary "Herland" created by Vingie E. Roe in *The Golden Tide* twenty years later. Regardless of whether or not Hooker or Roe would have accepted the label "feminist," the cumulative messages of both novels point in a feminist direction.

From about 1924 until the early 1940s, Cherry Wilson, who with her husband apparently lived in eastern Washington and northern Idaho,[5] contributed short stories, novelettes, and novels to *Western Story Magazine* and to other pulps. Some of her novels made it into hardcover,[6] but most of her fiction remains buried in scattered periodical files. In general, Wilson wrote according to the Western formula; one exception is "Stormy Dorn," a four-part serial in *Western Story Magazine* (1929). The protagonist, Cleo Craig, fits Leslie Fiedler's definition of the "Good Bad Girl." In this category Fiedler includes Henry James's Daisy Miller and the "hard-riding, hard-shooting . . . heroines of the dime novel"[7] with pure hearts beneath rough exteriors. Cleo is a professional rodeo rider, "bad" in that she hopes to steal a prized stallion and to seduce a hero type who loves someone else, "good" in that she matures, gives the man and her rival her blessing, and, having "made her biggest conquest—conquered herself," relinquishes hope of getting the stallion and looks forward to further challenges in "the rodeo game." The animal is given to her as a present, and neo-Freudians may speculate on the implications of a romance plot that leaves the heroine with a male horse but no prospective husband. However, the rebellious message encoded in the heroine's decision to pursue a career rather than marriage is surely clear. Readers expecting a conventional romance plot were probably satisfied by the hero's finally becoming engaged to his true love, a childhood sweetheart.

Wilson modified the formula more significantly in seven uncollected pieces about how a bunch of bachelor cowhands helped one another care for an orphaned child,[8] toward whom they have "a fiercely paternal attitude."[9] Cooperative child care by cowboys had figured in works by Bower, Maule, and Hooker, and if Wilson's stories on this theme were collected, they would constitute yet another example of the book-length domestic Western. The works by all four authors in this sub-subgenre imply that child-rearing may be done by groups of males; a mother is not indispensable. A corollary of this message is that if men will do child care, not every woman should be expected to accept homemaking and child-rearing as her main purpose in life. Another corollary is that in some cases the nuclear family may not be necessary for adequate child care—for those times (the mid-1920s), a radical attitude.

Of the pieces centered about Pard, as the child is nicknamed, the novella "Shootin'-up Sheriff" holds special interest as a fantasy about a town in which women have taken over the local administration. This plot is, as far as I know, unique among Westerns. The work is significant also because of the underlying political messages that make the story, from a feminist point of view, less dystopian than it may seem, if not quite utopian in the sense that, say, Charlotte Perkins Gilman's *Herland* is.

Two years before the story opens, the death of his mother in childbirth and of his father from a gunshot wound threw baby Pard into the lap of a cowboy, who thereupon abandoned his hell-raising bachelor ways and became a devoted foster parent, assisted by his bunkhouse comrades. The dying father told Hushaby—now so-called because he sings lullabies to the child—that he left money in a safe-deposit box to be invested in the child's name. Hushaby has finally gotten around to figuring that by not having put that money in a savings account he is losing Pard thirty cents a day in interest. The safe-box is in a bank in Bear Paw, the seat of an adjacent county. On a drunken spree, Hushaby had once shot out windows in that town and humiliated the lone banker in Bear Paw at gunpoint by making him sing and dance. Now he fears that the banker and the law would throw him in jail rather than honor his request concerning Pard's money. Jerry Paxton, sheriff of the county wherein Hushaby and his comrades reside, is a friend, and Hushaby asks Jerry to go with him to the Bear Paw bank and certify the cowboy's good faith and re-formed morality. Jerry agrees and goes into the town alone to scout the problem. He finds this once "wild, wide-open border settlement" (51) transformed. Bear Paw voters—ironically, because of Hushaby's destructive spree two years previously—have elected an all-female slate of city and county officials, including the sheriff and jailer. Laws previously ignored are now enforced, including the Volstead Act; the local speakeasy has been shut down. Further, "Smoking is frowned on. Swearing is a punishable offense. Gambling, rigidly banned. No form of night life is tolerated" (51). Only educational movies are shown. From Jerry's point of view, the town is dead. Moreover, the "veritable Amazon" of a sheriff is the wife of Rimrock, the banker Hushaby had humiliated, although relations between the couple have cooled because of the wife's new political role.

Overlooked for a few minutes, Pard strays into the office of the sheriff and is cuddled in a motherly fashion by that supposedly Amazonian official. Against Jerry's advice, Hushaby goes into the office after the child, and Jerry, sure that Hushaby has been arrested—and suffering too from the wounds inflicted by Mrs. Rimrock on his masculine vanity—impulsively shoots up the town, blasting lights and windows in a bloodless but destructive orgy. However, when Daisy, an attractive young female deputy, arrests him, he submits like a gentleman and is speedily locked in a cell.

Eventually the sight of his wife with the child in her arms and a "warm, maternal glow in her eyes" (59) revives Rimrock's marital affection and reawakens in both husband and wife the pain of having lost their only child years earlier. Now sympathetic to Hushaby's request, Rimrock quickly transfers Pard's money. A subsurface message in this reconciliation of the Rimrocks is that women can adopt masculine personae and perform competently in traditionally male roles without ceasing to be conventionally feminine in relation to their families. Mrs. Rimrock does her job adequately, and if Daisy isn't much help—Jerry Paxton easily escapes to freedom—well (such is the further implication), incompetent law personnel and escaping prisoners are common in towns run by men, including fictional towns in Westerns written by men.

Supported by most women's organizations, the Eighteenth Amendment had gone into effect in 1919, and by 1929, when "Shootin'-up Sheriff" appeared, the backlash that would lead to Prohibition's 1932 repeal was well under way. In "Sheriff," an overt political broadcast is that the "dry" regime is killing what's left of the color and excitement in the West (never mind that most of that excitement was created by and for males) and is bad for legitimate business besides. However, a covert message for feminists is that the women's movement's association with the temperance movement is a mistake in which women have gone too far in functioning as civilizers and as guardians of morality. Perhaps Wilson also felt, as did Caroline Lockhart, that the banning of booze invaded the recreational rights of women as well as of men.

The lightheartedly satirical tone of the entire narrative pokes fun at the terseness and tension of many formula Westerns—be it remembered that the genre was male-dominated. This tone is achieved partly through mock-epic passages—before taking the child into Bear Paw, Hushaby has "dread thoughts about what the morrow might bring"—and partly through redundant adverbs; for example, Hushaby "moaned piteously," "protested pathetically," and "cried fiercely," and Sheriff Paxton "snorted inelegantly." The satirical tone also implies that the supposed problem of women holding office is not serious at all; they can handle public responsibilities at least as well as can the men. The ending sends out a final dual message. On the one hand, readers are reassured that women really prefer private homemaking to public office, but on the other hand it is whispered that women deserve the freedom to make their own choices between civic and domestic roles and that public office should not be monopolized by males.

~~~~~

In one kind of formula Western, the plot was given a basis in actual historical events. Women writers played a considerable part in developing this variation. Frances Parker's *Winding Waters* (1909), based in large part on the Nez Percé campaign of 1877–1878, is an early example of history fictionalized by combination with the Western formula; another specimen is Forrestine Cooper Hooker's *When Geronimo Rode* (1924); yet another, Zane Grey's *The U. P. Trail*, is also an example of Frank Gruber's "epic of construction" plot type. Richard Etulain has noted that Ernest Haycox, beginning in 1937 with *Trouble Shooter* (based, like the *U. P. Trail*, on the construction of the Union Pacific railroad) and continuing with, among other historicals, *Bugles in the Afternoon* (about Custer), accentuated a growth in the frequency of historical Westerns.[10] However, Etulain says nothing about the women who earlier helped to start this trend, nor does he mention Vingie E. Roe's *The Golden Tide* (1940), in some aspects another example of this kind of Western. Two other women whose historical Westerns have been overlooked are Janet Cicchetti and Lillian Ressler; they collaborated under the pseudonym "Lillian Janet" in creating two novels, *Touchstone* (1947) and *The City Beyond Devil's Gate* (1950).[11]

Of these two historicals, *Touchstone* is the more ambitious and provocative. The authors try to combine the formula Western, with its emphasis on action and its simplistic values, with the panoramic family epic involving more complexity and realism (for example, John Galsworthy's *The Forsyte Saga* or Ruth Suckow's *The Folks*). "Janet" unfolds the story of two generations of the Delaney clan and their associates in the development of San Francisco and Sacramento during and after the gold rush of '49. In several ways the Western formula is debunked as well as followed. There are heroes and heroines, but they are flawed. A stereotyped villain turns into a hero but without reforming; a resolute pioneer woman is dehumanized by the struggle for wealth and status; and the economic basis of the marriage at closure is a house of prostitution. Women characters dominate the action; this phase of the West is viewed largely through their eyes, and extensive use is made of the double-voice strategy.

On the surface level, Western male chauvinism reaches an extreme when a stereotyped riverboat gambler tells two prostitutes, "Last night was last night! It's past!" (53). He then flings them bodily overboard from the steamer, whereon he wishes to preserve an appearance of gentility and elegance as a "cover" for his operations. Yet Steve Mallot, this bully of whores, later acts the part of a hero: He risks a shootout with a villain and eventually marries Treese Delaney, the heroine of this section of the novel. An ironic message encoded in Steve's character and actions is that in the Old West, evil, in the shape of pretense and male chauvinism, often prevailed; good and evil were often inextricably tangled, and the occasional apparent victories of the good were frequently achieved through concessions that would now be regarded with at least verbal and legal disapproval. Thus, the marriage of Steve and Treese, though it bids fair to be conventionally happy, is supported by the exploitation of "lost" women: Steve, the one-time caster-out of prostitutes, now employs such women as shills in his casino.

Much of the narrative concerns the mother of Treese, Agnes Delaney. Unfaithful to her weak-willed and boring husband, Agnes accepts from her lover a gift of capital, with which she enters the world of male pioneer entrepreneurship. Driven on a "warm current of confidence, starting from deep inside her" (61)—the true pioneer spirit—Agnes becomes the richest businessperson in Sacramento, outthinking, outdriving, and definitely outmanipulating male competitors and collaborators—and paying a price. Like Theodore Dreiser's Frank Cowperwood and Robert Penn Warren's Willie Stark, she pays for her wealth and status with forfeiture of romance, shrinkage of her personal horizon to obsession with power and wealth, and alienation of family and friends. An underlying message is that a successful woman must pay an even higher price than a successful male. Agnes loses her first two children in the cholera epidemic, to which she has exposed them through her business-motivated move to Sacramento, and her capacity for mother-love is further denied—self-denied—in her socially and economically motivated manipulation of Treese, the surviving daughter, into a disastrous marriage. What's left of Agnes's maternal affection is rejected by Treese herself when she defies her mother and breaks with her villainous and cowardly husband to wed the gambler Steve.

❧

Like the other writers examined in this study, the five introduced in this chapter were inspired by the Old West yet disturbed by the oppression of women therein. They expressed that disturbance in works that, despite qualifying loosely as formula Westerns, contained subsurface protests against patriarchal ideals of womanhood and imputations in favor of initiative and independence on the part of women. Two of these authors, Hooker and Wilson, pointed toward alternatives to the nuclear family, and all five writers presented heroines who dominated the narratives and moved the plots. Further, in trying to fit their dissenting viewpoints and their depictions of active heroines into the Western formula, these authors significantly enriched the hitherto neglected subgenre of Westerns by women.

8

RECAPITULATION AND CONCLUSIONS

Why did the West of formula fiction appeal to some women authors as subject matter in spite of its dominance by men? For Bower and Roe, one answer may be that they grew up in the West of the open range during the period when this West was passing from reality into history and myth. For Lockhart, Morrow, and Burt, an answer may be that they discovered it as adults during or shortly after that period. Two of these three, Morrow and Burt, came West because that's where their husbands' work happened to be.

Further, once each of the women introduced in this book decided to write mass-market fiction about the West and found the developing formula for the popular Western at hand, her choice, at least in retrospect, seems natural. In their private lives, some of them were outspoken feminists, but the decision to write formula Westerns made each of them—ex officio, so to speak—a feminist pioneer on a frontier possibly even more strongly dominated by men than the real, historical frontier. Little wonder, then, that in their novels these writers bent, warped, wrenched, and twisted the formula, giving more prominence, freedom, and status to women characters than male writers in this genre commonly allowed them and conveying feminist feelings and ideas through other strategies.

Often the heroine functioned as protagonist, a placement found only occasionally in Westerns by men. The heroines created by women commonly took the initiative and in so doing moved the plot rather than functioning merely as love objects, victims, servants, informants, and inspirers of men—in short, as mere accessories or occasions for men's actions. Frequently heroines performed in roles traditionally reserved for men, often because a father was dead or, if living, inadequate.

The lone, hard-beset heroine as protagonist had been a main aspect of the domestic/sentimental novel. Several other aspects of this genre were also incorporated into the Westerns of women authors. One such feature was the defective father, another an emphasis on family life and indoor settings. In women's Westerns the frequency of scenes within the four walls of a domestic establishment considerably surpasses that of such scenes in works by men. A few women authors even turned the cattle ranch from a rendezvous for footloose and hard-bitten cowboys into a center for an extended family.

Yet another element in the domestic novel had been the image of the Ideal Real Woman, a figure associated with physical fitness, self-reliance, some formal education, multiple skills, a cautious approach to marriage, and a claim to companionship after that event. This idea may have disappeared from popular letters some time after 1880.[1] However, it rose again in Westerns, especially in those by women, although modified by the requirement of the genre for fast pacing—a fast pace demanded a speedy falling in love.

The partial domestication of the Western also included a dearth of gunplay. Outdoors and in nondomestic establishments such as saloons, the women writers provide plenty of physical action, including horsemanship, flight and pursuit, storms, floods, stampedes, and rough-and-tumble fistfighting, usually though not exclusively among males; however, except in a few of Roe's narratives and in some of Bower's later novels, shootouts are rare. This rarity amounts to an implicit rejection of the six-gun mystique. John G. Cawelti's generalizations about the pistol and prowess therewith as basic identification marks of the Western hero seem inapplicable to most women's versions of this figure.

Westerns by women carried another message by omission. In Westerns by men, a variation of the romance plot had the hero riding over the horizon and retaining his freedom and mobility (although he often left behind a second-lead hero and a heroine whose coming together he had helped bring about). In preserving the hero's total freedom, including his sexual freedom, and in either leaving the heroine alone with love unrequited (her feelings don't really matter) or having her wed a man inferior to the hero (one man is as good as another for purposes of getting the heroine married off), male authors exemplified the formula stress on male bonding. Cawelti has noted that "however much he may be alienated from the town, the Western hero almost never appears without some kind of membership in a group of males."[2] My supposition is that women ignored this sort of ending because they opposed the views just indicated parenthetically.

As a strategy for conveying unpopular feelings and ideas, the double-voiced discourse, or palimpsestic text, was employed by these women authors in various ways. Making the heroine the protagonist was in itself one of these ways, and it was especially effective if she also moved the plot by direct action, for instance, by rescuing the hero—another rebellious strategy. The mere ranking of a woman as protagonist insinuated that women deserve as much or more attention than men in the fictional West (and maybe in real life, too), and having the heroine rescue a man reinforced that insinuation. Still another implied note from underground came whenever the romance plot was liberalized by the suggestion of alternatives to the heroine's routine journey into homemaking and motherhood. Even if the heroine was not the protagonist, any woman author who presented a physically active and mentally vigorous heroine thereby downgraded the dogma that woman's place was in the home to the status of an idea open to discussion and therefore to question.

Other forms of whispered dissent in women's Westerns included verbal irony, critical analogies, treatment of the Other Woman with unconventional leniency, and putting minor characters into the time-honored role of shrewd jester or wise fool who, being female and/or otherwise inferior, could utter unpleasant truths and not necessarily be taken seriously. Examples include the alcoholic sheepherder in *The Lady Doc,* the Apache confidante of Rhoda Tuttle in *The Heart of the Desert,* and several members in each of the Flying U, Diamond H, and Triangle Z happy families.

❦

In view of the material introduced in this book, revision of certain conclusions drawn by previous students of the Western and of popular culture in general seems in order. Propositions by John G. Cawelti, Frances B. Cogan, Daryl Jones, Henry Nash Smith, C. L. Sonnichsen, and Jane Tompkins have already been discussed. Annette Kolodny's approach in *The Lay of the Land* also needs re-examination. Kolodny claims that American pastoral literature "hailed the essential femininity of the terrain" and that at the core of the "American pastoral vocabulary" was a "yearning to know and to respond to the landscape as feminine, a yearning that I have labeled as the uniquely American 'pastoral impulse.' "[3] Among the women's Westerns investigated, I have not found consistent yearnings of this sort; these women are just as apt to find the landscape masculine as feminine. For example, in Hooker's *The Long, Dim Trail,* Katherine Glendon, in this passage surely speaking for the author, sees the desert as "masculine country" (40); some characters in Roe's novels see the landscape as masculine, and some see it as feminine.[4] In *Still Jim,* Morrow makes the desert a part of nature and denotes both entities with feminine pronouns, but in her *The Heart of the Desert* the landscape indicated in the title is personified by the hero. In Burt's *This Woman and This Man,* the heroine personifies the West, but elsewhere Burt associates the Western landscape with masculinity.[5]

More important than second-guessing previous commentators (though I hope this book is more than a set of second guesses) is the observation that a frequent feature of Westerns by women is the conflict between male and female drives within the heroine. I have tried to resist a reductionist temptation—in this case, to reduce the varied motivations of a number of characters to a single yin-yang polarity— but the conflict is there. According to the formula, self-reliance, the enjoyment of outdoor activities such as riding and shooting, the will to power, and the lure of achievement are masculine motivations, whereas inclinations toward morality, law, romantic love, home, and parenthood are feminine. Billy Louise MacDonald, heroine of Bower's *The Ranch at the Wolverine* (1914), feels the clash between "the Bill of me" and "the Louise of me" (3). She manages the small family ranch better than had her late father but settles at the end for marriage and in-house management. Lockhart's fighting shepherdess experiences internal strife between a need for love and the desire for material success and social revenge. In *Black Belle* and *The Divine Egotist*, Roe stresses the heroines' respect for law and order and their countervailing enjoyment of power, and Burt in *The Tall Ladder* emphasizes how Julia Oliphant's yearning for love and for an orderly ranch life clashes with the Napoleonic will to power inherited from her father. This sort of conflict is another aspect by which women's Westerns may be identified as a distinct subgenre within but not merged with the far more numerous Westerns by men.

Certain examples of ground-breaking by women authors of early Westerns rate mention if only because these experiments were symptomatic of American women's progress toward liberation during the early twentieth century. The most noteworthy of these pioneering efforts may be Caroline Lockhart's Dr. Emma Harpe, possibly the first lesbian in hardcover American fiction. Another is the marriage of a white heroine with a full-blood Native American in Morrow's *The Heart of the Desert* (1912). Yet another is Bower's Dr. Della Whitmore, probably the earliest woman physician in a formula Western. Dr. Harpe may well have been the second (and was probably the first to perform an abortion); Dr. Sonya Saverin in Roe's *Flame of the Border* (1933) may have been the third. One more early experiment is Kate Cathrew in Roe's *Nameless River* (1923), possibly the first "bad" woman outside of the dime novel to function as protagonist and to run a ranch competently and very likely the last to do either until Zane Grey's *The Maverick Queen* (1950).

Why have Westerns written by women been largely neglected? A tempting answer is simply because these works were indeed authored by women. However, Western fiction was for fast reading and quick forgetting; its writers' reputations were ephemeral regardless of gender. Of formula Western writers well known in the 1920s and 1930s, only Zane Grey still has a more or less familiar name. Reprints of novels by Frederick Faust, usually bearing his favorite pseudonym of Max Brand, may be seen on paperback racks occasionally, as may resurrected works of William MacLeod Raine and a very few others of that vintage. Of writers who began publishing in the 1940s, only Louis L'Amour remains well known to the general public. Westerns by a few authors who ended their writing careers in the 1940s or 1950s reappear sporadically, most of them titles by Henry Wilson Allen (Will Henry, Clay Fisher), Frederick D. Glidden (Luke Short), Ernest Haycox, and Joseph Wayne (Wayne D. Overholser). The women authors reintroduced in this book share neglect with several dozen, perhaps many more, male novelists whose work circulated briefly and soon sank into oblivion.

Like most of the male authors, the female authors underwent neglect by filmmakers. True, *Chip of the Flying U* was adapted for the screen four times; three of Caroline Lockhart's novels inspired movies, and *The Heart of the Desert* was also filmed, as were several of Vingie E. Roe's fictions. However, no characters based on fiction by women gave moviegoers and box-office accountants the thrills provided year after year by, say, the sixty-six Hopalong Cassidy films or the male-originated productions in which, among others, Bill Hart, Tom Mix, Hoot Gibson, Gary Cooper, and John Wayne appeared as stars. However, the robust, aggressive heroines of the women writers may be seen as foremothers of a type that emerged only in a new cultural milieu, that of World War II, and in movies reflecting that culture—and featuring, in the words of Sandra Kay Schackel, "the woman who can take care of herself and expects to do so."[6] Will Wright has commented that some post-World War II movies included women who were "no longer representatives of society requiring protection and exuding morality."[7] He cites *Johnny Guitar,* in which the "good" woman kills the "bad" woman in a private gun battle, and *El Dorado,* in which the heroine "dresses like a man, carries a gun, and kills the arch-villain in the final shootout, saving Cole Thornton's life."[8] In the final scene of *Johnny Guitar,* the heroine has also changed into men's shirt and pants.

Like Vingie Eve Roe's Lola, who kills a panther and leaves a note resembling Daniel Boone's, and like the same author's Belle Dawson, who wipes out the villain and in so doing saves the hero's life, these film heroines replaced the heroes in providing their own protection. Schackel discusses the expanded role of the heroine in several movies of the 1970s, including *Comes a Horseman* (wherein Jane Fonda stars as an independent small rancher), but she also cautions that "because men have most often written and directed Westerns, the films view women from a male perspective that emphasizes the male hero. . . . the frontier West was perceived by many as a masculine experience."[9] Even so, one may claim that most of the heroines created for print by the authors introduced in this study foreshadowed any partial emancipation of Western women that may have taken place in other media. These authors went further and represented the frontier West as an experience that could also be feminine.

Conclusions arrived at through any research may be significant in part because they pose new problems and suggest new opportunities for further research. For example, in *West of Everything*, Jane Tompkins concludes that, in film as well as in fiction, "the Western doesn't have anything to do with the West as such. It isn't about the encounter between civilization and the frontier. It is about men's fear of losing their mastery, and hence their identity, both of which the Western tirelessly reinvents."[10] Tompkins's conclusion, which I think is valid, has raised the question of how certain women writers of fiction could and did operate in the medium of the formula Western novel. I have attempted to outline how these writers not only participated in creating and sustaining the Western genre but in so doing created a subgenre of their own.

NOTES

Introduction

1.   Lillian S. Robinson, "Treason Our Text: Feminist Challenges to the Literary Canon," in *The New Feminist Criticism: Essays on Women, Literature, and Theory,* ed. Elaine Showalter (New York: Pantheon, 1985), 109. Omissions mine.

2.   Jane Tompkins, *West of Everything: The Inner Life of Westerns* (New York: Oxford University Press), 41–42. Her statement modifies an earlier assertion that Westerns "have always been written by men." See her "West of Everything," *South Atlantic Quarterly* 86 (1987): 371.

3.   Henry Nash Smith, *Virgin Land: The American West as Symbol and Myth* (1950; reprint, New York: Vintage Books, 1957), 126–135; and Daryl Jones, *The Dime Novel Western* (Bowling Green: Bowling Green University Popular Press, 1978), 4–5.

4.   Nina Baym, *Women's Fiction: A Guide to Novels by and About Women 1820–1870* (Ithaca: Cornell University Press, 1978), 11. Omissions mine.

5.   Frances B. Cogan, *All-American Girl: The Ideal of Real Womanhood in Mid-Nineteenth-Century America* (Athens: University of Georgia Press, 1989), 257. For the True Woman see Barbara Welter, *Dimity Convictions: The American Woman in the Nineteenth Century* (Athens: Ohio University Press, 1976), 21–41.

6.   Rachel Blau DuPlessis, *Writing Beyond the Ending: Narrative Strategies of Twentieth-Century Women Writers* (Bloomington: Indiana University Press, 1985), 5.

7.   Cogan, *All-American Girl,* 138–140.

8.   Elaine Showalter, "Women's Time, Women's Space: Writing the

History of Feminist Criticism," *Tulsa Studies in Women's Literature* 3 (Spring/Fall 1984): 39.

9. Elaine Showalter, "Feminist Criticism in the Wilderness," in *The New Feminist Criticism,* ed. Showalter, 266.

10. Sandra M. Gilbert and Susan Gubar, *The Madwoman in the Attic: The Woman Writer and the Nineteenth-Century Literary Imagination* (New Haven: Yale University Press, 1979), 73.

11. Tompkins, *West of Everything,* 42.

12. Saul David, "The West of Haycox Westerns," *Roundup* 12 (May 1964): 4. See also Tompkins, *West of Everything,* 39–40.

13. Christine Bold, *Selling the Wild West: Western Fiction 1860 to 1960* (Bloomington: Indiana University Press), 76; see also 91–104. Faust's favorite pseudonym was "Max Brand."

14. John A. Dinan, *The Pulp Western: A Popular History of the Western Fiction Magazine in America* (San Bernardino: Borgo Press, 1983), 14.

15. Frank Gruber, *The Pulp Jungle* (Los Angeles: Sherbourne Press, 1967), 184–186.

Chapter One

1. John R. Milton, *The Novel of the American West* (Lincoln: University of Nebraska Press, 1980), 14; John G. Cawelti, *The Six-Gun Mystique* (Bowling Green: Bowling Green State University Popular Press, 1971), 34–35.

2. Russel B. Nye, *The Unembarrassed Muse: The Popular Arts in America* (New York: Dial Press, 1970), 301–302.

3. Henry Nash Smith, *Virgin Land: The American West as Symbol and Myth* (Cambridge: Harvard University Press, 1950; reprint, New York: Vintage Books, 1957), 135. See also 126–135 as well as Daryl Jones, *The Dime Novel Western* (Bowling Green: Bowling Green State University Popular Press, 1978), 156–162.

4. Smith, *Virgin Land,* 126.

5. Jackson Gregory, *Redwood and Gold* (New York: Dodd, Mead, 1929); Vingie E. Roe, *Black Belle Rides the Uplands* (Garden City: Doubleday, Doran and Co., 1935).

6. Frances B. Cogan, "Weak Fathers and Other Beasts: An Examination of the American Male in Domestic Novels 1850–1870," *American Studies* 25 (Fall 1984): 5–20.

7. Helen Waite Papashvily, *All the Happy Endings: A Study of the Domestic Novel in America, the Women Who Wrote It, the Women Who Read It in the Nineteenth Century* (Port Washington, NY: 1956; reprint, New York: Harper &

Row, 1972), 75–94. I have relied on Papashvily and on Herbert Ross Brown, *The Sentimental Novel in America* (Durham: Duke University Press, 1940); William Wasserstrom, *Heiress of All the Ages: Sex and Sentiment in the Genteel Tradition* (Minneapolis: University of Minnesota Press, 1959); Earnest Ernest, *The American Eve in Fact and Fiction 1775–1914* (Urbana: University of Illinois Press, 1974); and Joyce Shaw Peterson, "Working Girls and Millionaires: The Melodramatic Novels of Laura Jean Libby," *American Studies* 24 (Spring 1983): 19–35.

8. Elaine Showalter, *A Literature of Their Own: British Women Novelists from Brontë to Lessing* (Princeton: Princeton University Press, 1977), 152. Omissions mine.

9. Owen Wister, *Members of the Family* (1911; reprint, New York: Macmillan Co., 1923), 15.

10. Lee Ann Johnson, "Mary Hallock Foote," *American Women Writers: A Critical Reference Guide from Colonial Times to the Present* (New York: Frederick Ungar, 1980), 60–62.

11. Mary Hallock Foote, *A Touch of Sun and Other Stories* (Boston: Houghton Mifflin Co., 1903), 128.

12. Owen Wister, *Lin McLean* (1897; reprint, New York: A. L. Burt Co., 1907), 59.

13. Nye, *Unembarrassed Muse*, 289.

14. John L. Cobbs, *Owen Wister,* Twayne United States Authors Series, 475 (Boston: Twayne Publishers, 1983), 16.

15. Owen Wister to Sarah Butler Wister [mother], July 5, 1902, unnumbered letter in *Owen Wister Out West*, ed. Fanny Kemble Wister (Chicago: University of Chicago Press, 1958).

16. Emerson Hough, *The Passing of the Frontier,* quoted in John D. Unruh, *The Plains Across: The Overland Emigrants and the Trans-Mississippi West 1840–1890* (Urbana: University of Illinois Press, 1979), 25. Omissions mine.

17. Elizabeth Ammons, *Conflicting Stories: American Women Writers at the Turn Into the Twentieth Century* (New York: Oxford University Press, 1992).

18. Other novels by Marah Ellis Ryan with Western settings include *That Girl Montana* (1901), *Told in the Hills* (1905), *For the Soul of Rafael* (1906), *Indian Love Letters* (1907), and *The Flute of the Gods* (1909). Other fiction by Florence Finch Kelly with Western settings includes *The Delafield Affair* (1909)—a novel—and *Emerson's Wife and Other Western Stories* (1911).

19. See also Frances Parker, *Winding Waters: The Story of a Long Trail and Strong Hearts* (1909), a novel inspired by the Nez Percé campaign of 1877–1878.

20.   Alfred Henry Lewis, *Wolfville* (New York: Frederick A. Stokes, 1897); *Sandburrs* (New York: Frederick A. Stokes, 1900); *Wolfville Days* (New York: Frederick A. Stokes, 1902); *Wolfville Nights* (New York: Frederick A. Stokes, 1902); *The Black Lion Inn* (New York: R. H. Russell Co., 1903); *Wolfville Folks* (New York: D. Appleton and Co., 1908); *Faro Nell and Her Friends* (New York: G. W. Dillingham Co., 1913). A selection of Lewis's Wolfville pieces is available in *Wolfville Yarns of Alfred Henry Lewis,* ed. by Rolfe Humphries and John Humphries (Ravenna: Kent State University Press, 1968). For an overview of Lewis and his work, see Abe C. Ravitz, *Alfred Henry Lewis,* Boise State University Western Writers Series, 32 (Boise: Boise State University Press, 1978).

21.   Lewis, *Wolfville Yarns,* 464–501.

22.   Lewis, *Wolfville Nights,* 65.

23.   Richard W. Etulain, "A Dedication to . . . Zane Grey 1872–1939," *Arizona and the West* 12 (1970): 217–220. Omissions mine.

24.   Teresa Jordan, *Cowgirls: Women of the American West* (Garden City: Doubleday Anchor Books, 1982), 292. Omissions mine.

25.   Jackson Gregory and James B. Hendryx were among the few male authors who occasionally depicted active female protagonists. For example, see the former's *Judith of Blue Lake Ranch* (1917; reprint, New York: Grosset & Dunlap, 1920), and the latter's *The Yukon Kid* (1930; reprint, New York: Triangle Books, 1943). However, the heroines in both novels wind up engaged to the heroes.

26.   Anne Falke cites a few male authors who in the 1950s and 1960s manipulated the formula especially in the treatment of heroines. See her "The Art of Convention: Images of Women in the Modern Western Novels of Henry Wilson Allen," *North Dakota Quarterly* 42 (Spring 1974): 17–27. Allen, who used the pseudonyms of Will Henry and Clay Fisher, began publishing in the 1950s.

Chapter Two

1.   B. M. Bower [Bertha Muzzy Sinclair Cowan], *Flying U Ranch* (1912; reprint, New York: Grosset & Dunlap, n.d.), 47. A reference to the home ranch of the Happy Family.

2.   Douglas Branch, *The Cowboy and His Interpreters* (New York: D. Appleton and Co., 1926), 241. Branch's evaluation of Bower's fiction is on the whole favorable. J. Frank Dobie had one sentence for Bower in *Guide to Life and Literature in the Southwest* (Austin: University of Texas Press, 1943), 61. He said, "This [*Chip of the Flying U*] and some other Bower novels are al-

most—but not quite—as good as those of E. M. Rhodes." Eugene Manlove Rhodes was Dobie's favorite Western fictionist.

3. The figure of 2 million is my extrapolation, based on the publisher's claim in the front matter of B. M. Bower, *A Starry Night* (Boston: Little, Brown and Co., 1939) that 1,740,596 copies of her books had been sold in twenty years. For the estimates concerning Grey and L'Amour, see respectively John G. Cawelti, *The Six-Gun Mystique* (Bowling Green: Bowling Green State University Popular Press, 1971), 2, and Robert Phillips, *Louis L'Amour: His Life and Trails* (1989; reprint, New York: Knightsbridge Publishing Co., 1990), 11.

4. Orrin Engen, *Writer of the Plains (A Biography of B. M. Bower)* (Culver City: Pontine Press, 1973). See also Russel B. Nye, *The Unembarrassed Muse: The Popular Arts in America* (New York: Dial Press, 1970), 291–292; Stanley R. Davison, "The Author Was a Lady," *Montana: The Magazine of Western History* 23 (Spring 1973): 215; and Roy W. Meyer, "B. M. Bower: The Poor Man's Wister," in *The Popular Western: Essays Toward a Definition*, ed. Richard W. Etulain and Michael T. Marsden (Bowling Green: Bowling Green State University Popular Press, 1974): 666/24–679/37.

5. Engen, *Writer of the Plains*, iii, 2, 42–45.

6. Annette Kolodny, *The Land Before Her: Fantasy and Experience of the American Frontiers, 1630–1860* (Chapel Hill: University of North Carolina Press, 1984), 203. See also Annette Kolodny, *The Lay of the Land: Metaphor As Experience and History in American Life and Letters* (Chapel Hill: University of North Carolina Press, 1975), 5.

7. Tania Modleski, *Feminism Without Women* (New York and London: Routledge, 1991), 77.

8. Elaine Showalter, *A Literature of Their Own: British Women Novelists from Brontë* to Lessing (Princeton: Princeton University Press, 1977), 152.

9. Elaine Showalter, "Feminist Criticism in the Wilderness," in *The New Feminist Criticism: Essays on Women, Literature, and Theory*, ed. Elaine Showalter (New York: Pantheon Books, 1985), 266; Sandra Gilbert and Susan Gubar, *The Madwoman in the Attic: Women Writers and the Nineteenth-Century Literary Imagination* (New Haven: Yale University Press, 1979), 73.

10. Engen, *Writer of the Plains*, 2. I am indebted to Engen's booklet for all biographical and bibliographical information except where otherwise indicated.

11. Stanley J. Kunitz and Howard Haycraft, *Twentieth Century Authors*, sixth printing (New York: H. W. Wilson Co., 1966), 160.

12. Engen, *Writer of the Plains*, 4.

13. Engen, *Writer of the Plains*, 50.

14. B. M. Bower, *Rodeo* (1928; reprint, New York: Triangle Books, 1943), 24.

15. B. M. Bower, *The Flying U's Last Stand* (1915; reprint, New York: Grosset & Dunlap, n.d.), 6.

16. B. M. Bower, "Chip of the Flying U," *Popular Magazine* (October 1904), according to Engen, *Writer of the Plains,* 30.

17. Bower, *Flying U Ranch,* 27–30. Cf. B. M. Bower, *The Family Failing* (Boston: Little, Brown, and Co., 1941), 90–92.

18. Bower, *Flying U Ranch,* 41.

19. Honoré Willsie [Morrow], "Breaking the Blue Roan," *Everybody's Magazine* 45 (December 1921): 16.

20. In "The Author Was a Lady" (6), Davison says that one of Russell's paintings may have inspired the author's description of Chip and Della's drawing.

21. June Sochen, *The New Woman: Feminism in Greenwich Village 1910–1920* (New York: Quadrangle Books, 1972). ix.

22. George H. Lorimer, *Letters from a Self-Made Merchant to His Son* (Boston: Small, Maynard & Co., 1902), 310–311. Omissions mine.

23. Elaine Showalter, "Review Essay," *Signs* 1 (Winter 1975): 435. Quoted in Gilbert and Gubar, *Madwoman in the Attic,* 77–78. Omissions mine.

24. Mary K. Maule, *The Little Knight of the X Bar B* (Boston: Lothrop, Lee & Shepard Co., 1910). The book is not a juvenile. For a list of Cherry Wilson's tales about "Pard," see Chapter 7, note 8.

25. B. M. Bower, *The Lonesome Trail* (1909; reprint, New York: Grosset & Dunlap, n.d.), 167. The novella from which these were taken—"The Lamb," 165–200—has been republished in a somewhat condensed version in *She Won the West: An Anthology of Western and Frontier Stories by Women,* ed. Marcia Muller and Bill Pronzini (New York: William Morrow and Co., 1985), 101–118. The editorial headnote about Bower (99) contains several errors of fact.

26. Bower, *The Flying U's Last Stand,* 6.

27. *Ibid.,* 58.

28. Bower, *The Family Failing,* 154–178. The book is a collection of loosely interconnected episodes, of which Pink's impersonation at the masquerade ball encompasses Chapters 14 through 16.

29. Rachel Blau DuPlessis, *Writing Beyond the Ending: Narrative Strategies of Twentieth-Century Women Writers* (Bloomington: Indiana University Press, 1985).

30. According to Engen's "Chronology" in *Writer of the Plains* (no pagi-

nation), film versions of *Chip* were released in 1914 (a production starring Tom Mix), 1920, 1926, and 1939. Other films known to have been adapted from Bower fiction were *The Galloping Devil* (1920, adapted from *The Happy Family*); *The Wolverine* (1921, from *The Ranch of the Wolverine*); *The Flying U Ranch* (1927, from *Flying U Ranch*); *King of the Rodeo* (1929, from *Rodeo*); and *Points West* (1929, from *Points West*). See Robert B. Connelly, ed., *Silent Films 1910–1936* (Chicago: Cinébooks, 1986), and Kenneth W. Munden, ed., *The American Film Institute Catalog of Motion Pictures Produced in the United States: Feature Films 1921–1930* (New York: R. R. Bowker Co., 1988), 125–26, 311.

Chapter Three

1. Anthony Channel Hilfer, *The Revolt from the Village 1912–1930* (Chapel Hill: University of North Carolina Press, 1969).

2. Kathryn Wright, "Author Caroline Lockhart Dies in Cody at 91 Years," *Billings* [Mont.] *Gazette* December 26, 1962: 2, 5. Actually Lockhart lived to be ninety-two.

For all biographical information about this author, except where otherwise stated, I have relied on the following series of articles by Frank Boyette in the *Cody* [Wyo.] *Enterprise*: "Courageous or stubborn? Caroline Lockhart wrangles control of 1920s Cody *Enterprise*, quickly becomes champion of 'Wet' forces" (August 21, 1989: A10); "Lockhart attacks Newton's candidates" (August 23, 1989: B1, B2); "Publisher Lockhart, prosecutor Goppert," (August 28, 1989: B1, B8); "Lockhart, Goppert lock horns again" (August 30, 1989: B1, B2).

3. *Cody Enterprise* (August 21, 1989): A10.

4. Agnes Wright Spring, "White Woman-Boss," *Sunset* (October 1923): 41.

5. *Cody Enterprise* (August 30, 1989): B2.

6. Sandra M. Gilbert and Susan Gubar, *The Madwoman in the Attic: The Woman Writer and the Nineteenth-Century Literary Imagination* (New Haven: Yale University Press, 1979), 77–78.

7. B. M. Bower, "Miss Martin's Mission," in *The Happy Family* (1910; reprint, New York: Grosset & Dunlap, n.d.), 61–89.

8. Jean Carwile Masteller, "The Woman Doctors of Howells, Phelps, and Jewett: The Conflict of Marriage and Career," in *Critical Essays on Sarah Orne Jewett*, ed. Gwen C. Nagel (Boston: G. K. Hall, 1984), 135–147.

9. Richard Harrison Shryock, *Medicine in America: Historical Essays* (Baltimore: Johns Hopkins University Press, 1960), 160. Reminiscing about

her life on a frontier ranch in New Mexico, Agnes Morley Cleaveland wrote in *No Life for a Lady* (Boston: Houghton Mifflin Co., 1941), 233, concerning a woman who practiced medicine without a license: "When I recall some of those early-day examples of medical practice on the part of the few doctors who came into our midst with licenses, I think I should have felt quite as safe under the ministrations of Mrs. Stevens."

10. Caroline Lockhart, *The Lady Doc* (Philadelphia: J. B. Lippincott Co., 1912), 17–19. The operation—forbidden by the friend's husband—is not specifically designated, but its nature is clearly implied. According to Ruth Miller Elson, *Myths and Mores in American Best Sellers 1865–1965* (New York: Garland, 1985), 50, abortion was first mentioned in American fiction by Donald Henderson Clarke in a novel entitled *Louis Beretti* (1929).

11. Lucille Patrick Hicks, *Caroline Lockhart: Liberated Lady—1870–1962* (Cheyenne: Pioneer Printing and Stationery Co., 1984), 38.

12. Gilbert and Gubar, *Madwoman*, 78.

13. Review of *The Fighting Shepherdess*, by Caroline Lockhart, *Springfield Republican* (August 3, 1919): 17.

14. In "Working Girls and Millionaires: The Melodramatic Romances of Laura Jean Libby," *American Studies* 24 (Spring 1983): 19–35; Joyce Shaw Peterson notes that this plot pattern occurs repeatedly in Libby's novels.

15. Harold Bell Wright, *The Winning of Barbara Worth* (Chicago: Book Supply Co., 1911), and *When a Man's a Man* (Chicago: Book Supply Co., 1916). Heroes of both novels are upper-class Easterners. That of the former is an engineer; of the latter, a playboy.

16. "Death Stills Pen of Caroline Lockhart," *Cody Enterprise* (August 2, 1962): 1, 4.

17. Robert B. Connelly, ed., *Silent Films 1910–1936* (Chicago: Ciné-books, 1986). According to this source, Lockhart's *The Man from the Bitter Roots* and *The Dude Wrangler*, as well as a short story, "The Man from Oregon," were also adapted for film. See also Patricia King Hanson and Alan Gerinson, eds., *The American Film Institute Catalog of Motion Pictures Produced in the United States: Feature Films 1911–1920* (Berkeley: University of California Press, 1988), 206, 276, 571.

18. Review of *"Me—Smith,"* by Caroline Lockhart, *New York Times* (March 19, 1911): 16. See also the review in *Review of Reviews* (June 1911): 43.

19. Review of *The Lady Doc*, by Caroline Lockhart, *New York Times* (October 27, 1912): 628.

20. D. L. M., review of *The Fighting Shepherdess*, by Caroline Lockhart,

Boston Transcript (March 20, 1919): 9; review of the same novel, *New York Times* (May 11, 1919): 24.

21.   Lockhart's preservation of a heroine's virginity by the sudden elimination of her new husband has at least one precedent in Westerns by women. The heroine of Frances Parker's *Marjie of the Lower Ranch* (Boston: C. M. Clark Publishing Co., 1904) is lured into marriage by a villain who is immediately shot in a saloon brawl.

Chapter Four

1.   Nina Baym, "Melodramas of Beset Manhood: How Theories of American Fiction Exclude Women Authors," *American Quarterly* 33 (1981): 139; Joanna Russ, "What Can a Heroine Do? Or Why Women Can't Write," in *Images of Women in Fiction: Feminist Perspectives,* ed. Susan Koppleman Cornillon (Bowling Green: Bowling Green State University Popular Press, 1973): 6.

2.   See *The Complete Poetical Works of Edmund Spenser,* ed. R.E. Neil Dodge (1908; reprint, Boston: Houghton Mifflin Co., 1936), 325–417.

3.   Vingie E. Roe, *Black Belle Rides the Uplands* (Garden City: Doubleday, Doran and Co., 1935), 3, 28; see also her "In Round Stone Valley," *Collier's Weekly* (February 23, 1918): 18; "Nameless River," Part One, *McCall's Magazine* (March 1923): 9; "The Lumberjack," *Everybody's Magazine* (December 1918): 83; "Black Thunder," *Collier's Weekly* (October 30, 1915): 22; "Surrender," Part Two, *Sunset* (April 1918): 28; *Flame of the Border* (Garden City: Doubleday, Doran and Co., 1933), 32, 98; and *A Woman of the Great Valley* (1956; reprint, London: Cassell, 1956), 74.

4.   Paul R. Eldridge, "The Incomparable Vingie," pp. 20–21, typescript in the Sonoma County [CA] Library, Cloverdale Regional Branch, Cloverdale, CA.

5.   Vingie E. Roe, "Shadows of Granite Ridge: White Ears on Guard," *Western Story Magazine* (October 6, 1923), 100–107. For the inscription by Daniel Boone see John Bakeless, *Master of the Wilderness: Daniel Boone* (New York: William Morrow, 1939), 32–33. The full inscription is: "D. Boon Cilled a Bar on Tree in the year 1760."

6.   Vingie E. Roe, "Shadows of Granite Ridge: The Desperate Bluff," *Western Story Magazine* (September 29, 1923): 96–107.

7.   B. B. Chapman, "A Letter from Vingie E. Roe," typescript, in "Scrapbook of Vingie E. Roe," Oklahoma State University Library, Stillwater, Oklahoma. Chapman dates the letter only by year, 1929.

8. Roe, "Vingie E. Roe By Herself,"*Sunset* (March 1918): 21.

9. Daryl Jones, *The Dime Novel Western* (Bowling Green: Bowling Green State University Popular Press, 1978), 146–147.

10. Roe, "Vingie E. Roe By Herself," 21. The "Epworth League" was at that time the name of the youth-oriented branch of the Methodist Episcopal Church.

11. Jane Tompkins, *West of Everything: The Inner Life of Westerns* (New York: Oxford University Press, 1992), 28–45. Tompkins claims that the Western, with its emphasis on justice through violence, rejected Christianity.

12. Roe, *Flame of the Border,* 181–182. Omissions mine. Much the same language is used in Roe, *Black Belle,* 206, 276.

13. Roe, "Nameless River," Part One, 32. The serialized version (in *McCall's,* March–June 1923) is used in this chapter because a copy of the book version was available to me only briefly.

14. "Mrs. Lawton Writes Novels While Husband Sweeps and Makes the Beds," *Medford* [OR] *Mail-Tribune* (February 25, 1912): 7. Clipping in possession of Jackson County Historical Society, Medford, OR.

15. "Mrs. Lawton Writes Novels,' 7; Chapman, "A Letter." For the Heck Thomas episode see "Vingie E. Roe recalls days at Carney," typescript, in "Scrapbook." The Roe collection at the Oklahoma State University Library also includes a copy of this author's *The Heart of Night Wind* that had been presented, according to a handwritten note on the flyleaf, to "That Seer, That Beckoner, Dr. A. G. Scott."

16. "Mrs. Lawton Writes Novels," 11; Robert W. Merten, "A Biographical Sketch of V. E. Roe," typescript, in Roe collection, OSU library.

17. "Mrs. Lawton Writes Novels," 7.

18. Merten, "Biographical Sketch." Merten was a cousin of Roe.

19. Jennie Harris Oliver, "Vingie E. Roe," *The Daily Oklahoman* (August 16, 1925), typescript, in "Scrapbook."

20. Jones, *The Dime Novel Western,* 144. Cf. Leslie A. Fiedler, *Love and Death in the American Novel,* revised edition (New York: Stein and Day, 1966), 296–312.

21. Anne Falke, "The Art of Convention: Images of Women in the Modern Western Novels of Henry Wilson Allen," *North Dakota Quarterly* 42 (Spring 1974): 18.

22. Frank Gruber, *The Pulp Jungle* (Los Angeles: Sherbourne Press, 1967), 185. See also Russel B. Nye, *The Unembarrassed Muse: The Popular Arts in America* (New York: Dial Press, 1970), 301.

23. Cf. Roe, "Nameless River," Part Five, 36, and Vingie E. Roe, *Name-*

less River (New York: Duffield and Co., 1923), 259. Omissions mine. Queasiness of a different sort from that operating at *McCall's* was shown by a reviewer who found the book "harmlessly inoffensive, a decidedly redeeming feature in these days of naturalistic fiction." See review of *Nameless River* by Vingie E. Roe, *Boston Transcript* (October 10, 1923): 4.

24. Jane Tompkins, "West of Everything," *South Atlantic Quarterly* 86 (Fall 1887): 361, 364. Cf. Tompkins, *West of Everything*, 31.

25. Roe, *Black Belle*, 34; see also Vingie E. Roe, *Tharon of Lost Valley* (1919; reprint, New York: Grosset & Dunlap, n.d.); "What Happened at El Rancho Verde," *Collier's Weekly* (December 18, 1915): 7–8, 30–31, 33–34; and "That Girl at Enright's," *Sunset* (July 1988): 27–30.

26. B. M. Bower, *The Heritage of the Sioux* (Boston: Little, Brown, and Co., 1916), 311–312; Zane Grey, *To the Last Man* (1922; reprint, New York: Harper & Row, 1950), 224–225; James B. Hendryx, *The Yukon Kid* (1933; reprint, New York: Triangle Books, 1943), 293; and Nelson Nye, "Gallows Bait," in Nelson Nye, *Wide Loop* (1935; reprint, Kensington [NY]: Zebra Books, 1978), 232–233; Will Henry [Henry Wilson Allen], *The Bear Paw Horses* (1973; reprint, New York: Bantam, 1980), 39.

27. Vingie E. Roe, "The Story of the Factor's Book," *Munsey's Magazine* (October 1906): 48–51. The jealous fiancée stakes out her betrothed for the vultures to devour alive. On learning that her suspicions of his fickleness had been unjustified, she loses her mind.

28. Diana Reep, *The Rescue and Romance: Popular Novels Before World War I* (Bowling Green: Bowling Green State University Popular Press, 1982), 7, 84, 100–102.

29. Pamela Herr, "Reformer," in *The Women Who Made the West: By the Western Writers of America* (1980; reprint, Avon Discus Books, 1981), 206. Roe probably knew about Asa Mercer's having brought groups of single women to the Pacific Northwest, primarily for matrimonial purposes, in 1864 and 1866, but I have found no indication that she made use of any documents relating to these expeditions. Mercer's endeavors and their results are summarized by Roberta Frye Watt, "The Mercer Girls," in *Four Wagons West: The Story of Seattle* (Portland [Oregon]: Metropolitan Press, 1931), 308–323. See also *Mercer's Belles: The Journal of a Reporter*, ed. Lenna A. Deutsch (Seattle: University of Washington Press, 1960).

30. In Vingie E. Roe, *Glory in the Gum Woods* (London: Cassell, 1937), the strong-minded mother of the heroine rescues a young woman from a brothel: "Never mind where I found her . . . hit took me an' two of 'cers of th' law t'git her out" (250). Omissions mine.

31. Rachel Blau DuPlessis, *Writing Beyond the Ending: Narrative Strategies*

of Twentieth-Century Women Writers (Bloomington: Indiana University Press, 1985), 5.

32. E.g., see Max Brand [Frederick Faust], *Silvertip's Chase* (1933; reprint, New York: Warner Books, 1975).

32. Roe may have published novel-length magazine or newspaper serials that have never gotten between book covers. No bibliography of Roe's work exists in print, and no attempt has been made, even by the Library of Congress, to assemble a complete set of her novels or to list her more than sixty short stories (my estimate). An "Author's Set" including twenty-seven of the possibly thirty-one Roe novels published in book form is in the OSU library. Some of these volumes are in poor condition, precluding circulation via interlibrary loan.

34. Of *The Heart of Night Wind* a reviewer wrote, "There is an inordinate amount of villainy that belongs to a lower level of literature and detracts much from the real interest in the story." See review of this novel, *New York Sun* (May 17, 1913): 3. On the other hand, about *Nameless River* one comment was, "The best of the story lies in its many eloquently written passages of nature description." See review of this work in the *New York Times* (July 23, 1923): 18.

35. "Mrs. Lawton Writes Novels," 11.

36. Chapman, "A Letter from Vingie E. Roe."

37. "Vingie E. Roe, 78, Novelist, Dies," *Cloverdale* [CA] *Reveille* (August 14, 1958): 1.

38. Richard Bertrand Dimmitt, *A Title Guide to the Talkies: A Comprehensive Listing of 16,000 Feature-Length Films from October, 1927, Until December, 1963* (New York: Scarecrow Press, 1965), 2: 1304. See also Kenneth W. Munden, ed. *The American Film Institute Catalog of Motion Pictures Produced in the United States: Feature Films 1921–1930* (New York: R. R. Bowker Company, 1971), 757, and Patricia King Hanson and Alan Gevinson, eds., *The American Film Institute Catalog of Motion Pictures Produced in the United States: Feature Films 1911–1920* (Berkeley: University of California Press, 1988), 737, 957, 1038. *Twilight* (1918) and *Wild Honey* (1918) were films adapted from Roe short stories with the same titles.

39. F.T. Cooper, review of *The Heart of Night Wind*, by Vingie E. Roe, *Bookman* 37 (May 1913): 339.

Chapter Five

1. Ernest E. Leisy, *The American Historical Novel* (Norman: University of Oklahoma Press, 1960), 139–60.

2. "Morrow, Mrs. Honoré Willsie," *Twentieth Century Authors*, ed. Stanley J. Kunitz and Howard Haycraft, 6th printing (New York: H. W. Wilson, 1966), 990. See also Abigail Ann Hamblen, Honoré Willsie Morrow," *American Woman Writers* (New York: Garland Publishing Co., 1977), 3, 225–26; and Robert E. Spiller, et al *Literary History of the United States,* 3rd edition, revised (New York: Macmillan Co., 1963), 321, 323, wherein Morrow's non-Western novel *Lydia of the Pines* (1917) is cited as a "picture of political graft dealing with the Indian lands of Minnesota" and her *We Must March* (1925) is mentioned along with other historical novels about the Pacific Northwest by various writers. Formula-Western novels by Morrow not discussed in my text are *Still Jim* (1915), *The Forbidden Trail* (1919), *The Enchanted Canyon* (1921), and *The Devonshers* (1924). Non-Western novels by Morrow not mentioned in my text include *Benefits Forgot* (1917), *The Splendor of God* (1929), *Tiger! Tiger!* (1930), *Yonder Sails the Mayflower* (1934), and *Let the King Beware* (1935). Historical novels about the West by Morrow that do not fall into the category of formula Western are *We Must March* (1925), *On to Oregon!* (a juvenile, 1926), *Beyond the Blue Sierra* (1932), and *Argonaut* (1933). An obituary notice appears in the *New York Times* (April 13, 1940); L17.

3. C. L. Sonnichsen, *From Hopalong to Hud: Thoughts on Western Fiction* (College Station: Texas A. & M. University Press, 1978), 68.

4. Diana Reep, *The Rescue and Romance: Popular Novels Before World War I* (Bowling Green: Bowling Green State University Popular Press, 1982), 7. Among the best-selling novels discussed by Reep are three Westerns: Owen Wister's *The Virginian*, Zane Grey's *The Lone Star Ranger,* and Harold Bell Wright's *The Winning of Barbara Worth.*

5. Arthur Margon, "Changing Modes of Heroism in Popular American Novels 1880–1920," *American Studies* 17 (Fall 1976): 71–86. Margon does not mention any of Morrow's novels, nor does he cite another early Western featuring an engineer as hero: Ednah Aiken's *The River* (Indianapolis: Bobbs-Merrill Co., 1914).

6. "Honoré Morrow, Writer on Lincoln," 17; Honoré Willsie, "The Adopted Mother," *Century* (September 1922): 654–668. For her views on the desirability that WASP mothers bear more children, see Honoré Willsie, "What Is an American?" Part II. *Collier's* (November 30, 1912): 17, 22, 24.

7. Patricia King Hanson and Alan Gevinson, eds., *The American Film Institute Catalog . . . Feature Films 1911–1920.* Berkeley: University of California Press, 1988), 761.

8. Honoré Willsie, "Breaking the Blue Roan," *Everybody's Magazine*

(December 1921): 8. Omissions mine. The editorial headnote distorts this piece by designating it, "The Search of a Man for Beauty, and How and Where He Found It." Thus, the story is taken away from the woman and given to the man.

9. Morrow wrote several essays about the development of her religious faith. These include "Chapters from Unwritten Autobiographies / III / Book Hunger," *Bookman* (May 1924): 306–310; "God in the Darkness,"*Cosmopolitan* (November 1927): 62–63, 164–168; "The Strangest Adventure a Woman Ever Had," *American Magazine* (January 1929): 24–27, 80, 82, 84, 86; and "I Learned About God from a Negress," *Cosmopolitan* (March 1929): 28–29, 144, 146, 148–150. The reference to herself as an "agnostic" occurs in *Prairie Gold, by Iowa Authors and Artists* (Chicago: The Reilly & Britton Co., 1917), 283. See also "Tragedy of a Godless Childhood," *Literary Digest* (March 31, 1923): 31–32.

10. W. H. Carruth, *Each in His Own Tongue and Other Poems* (New York: G. P. Putnam's Sons, 1907), 2–3. The first four lines quoted by Judith are: "A fire mist and a planet, / A crystal and a cell, / A jelly-fish and a saurian / And caves where cavemen dwell."

11. Anonymous review of *Judith of the Godless Valley* in *Current Opinion* (November 1922): 593.

12. Excluding sociological novels like Upton Sinclair's *The Jungle* and John Steinbeck's *The Grapes of Wrath,* Blotner discusses only novels that "deal with the overt, institutionalized politics of the officeholder, the candidate, the party official, or the individual who performs political acts as they are conventionally understood." Part of the discussion in one chapter, "The Young Knight," could apply to Willsie's Hugh Stewart, and part in another, "The Role of Women," fits the characterization and function of Mrs. Ellis, Hugh's campaign manager. See Joseph Blotner, *The Modern American Political Novel 1900–1960* (Austin: University of Texas Press, 1966), 8, 18–54, 164–190.

13. Helen Hunt Jackson [Saxe Holm], "Draxy Miller's Dowry," in *Saxe Holm's Stories: First Series* (New York: Charles Scribner's Sons, 1873), 2. Omissions mine.

14. *Delineator* (March 1918): 3.

15. Honoré Willsie, "What Is an American? Part II." *Collier's* (November 9, 1912): 13–14, 42.

16. Willsie, *Exile*, 113. Owen Wister in *The Virginian* specified that the heroine "was not a New Woman" (81). Whatever else Wister may have meant, he was implying that Molly Wood was uninvolved in politics.

17. Marcia Muller and Bill Pronzini, eds., *She Won the West: An Anthology*

of Frontier Stories by Women (New York: William Morrow and Co., 1985) includes an excerpt from one of B. M. Bower's Happy Family collections, "The Lamb of the Flying U" (101–118), but nothing by Morrow. Ironically, the firm that published this compilation was founded by William Morrow, second husband of the author under discussion, and after 1925 the company published all of her books. Vera Norwood and Janice Monk, eds., *The Desert Is No Lady* (New Haven: Yale University Press, 1987), likewise includes none of Morrow's work.

18.   Implied criticism of marriage as the exclusive goal for women may be found in some of Morrow's uncollected short pieces—for example, "The Schooling of Isabel Dawes, Spinster," *Delineator* (September 1914): 8, 41, 43; and "Desert Justice," *Everybody's Magazine* (September 1922): 99–134. In an article on "Women and Food Deterioration," *Collier's* (April 20, 1912): 22–25, Morrow had written that half of a woman's education should be aimed at enabling her to support herself.

19. Grant Overton, "She Pioneered in Novels," *The Mentor*, 15 (July 1927): 58.

Chapter Six

1.   Editorial headnote to Katharine Newlin Burt, "Herself," in *O. Henry Memorial Award Prize Stories of 1930*, ed. Blanche Colton Williams (Garden City: Doubleday, Doran and Co., 1930), 70.

2.   Burt's other Westerns are *"Q"* (1922), *A Man's Own Country* (1931), *This Woman and This Man* (1934), and *Men of Moon Mountain* (1938).

3.   Nathaniel Burt, *Jackson Hole Journal* (Norman: University of Oklahoma Press, 1983), 191–192.

4.   *Twentieth Century Authors*, "Burt, Mrs. Katharine Newlin," in Stanley J. Kunitz and Howard Haycroft, eds., 6th edition (New York: H. Wilson, 1966), 228.

5.   *Ibid.*

6.   Maxwell Struthers Burt, *The Diary of a Dude-Wrangler* (New York: Charles Scribner's Sons, 1924), 145.

7.   *Twentieth Century Authors.*

8.   Maxwell Struthers Burt's novels were: *The Interpreter's House* (1924), *The Delectable Mountains* (1927), and *Along These Streets* (1942). His short-story collections were: *John May and Other Stories* (1918), *Chance Encounter* (1921), and *They Could Not Sleep* (1928). His life and career have been surveyed by Raymond C. Phillips, Jr. in *Struthers Burt*, Boise State University Western Writers Series 56 (Boise: Boise State University Press, 1983). So

far, Katharine Newlin Burt is unrepresented in that series and as far as I know, unexamined in any other scholarly publications.

9. Nathaniel Burt, *Jackson Hole,* 193.

10. Francis B. Cogan, "Weak Fathers and Other Beasts: An Examination of the American Male in Domestic Novels, 1850–1870," *American Studies* 25 (Fall 1984): 5–20.

11. Review of *The Branding Iron,* by Katharine Newlin Burt, *Nation* 109 (August 23, 1920): 252. Theodocia Walton, in an untitled brief in "Interesting Westerners," *Sunset* (April 1921): 47, refers to *The Branding Iron* and "Snow Blindness" [sic] as having been filmed.

12. Diana Reep, *Rescue and Romance: Popular Novels Before World War I* (Bowling Green: Bowling Green State University Popular Press, 1982), 100–102.

Chapter Seven

1. Diana Reep, *Rescue and Romance: Popular Novels Before World War I* (Bowling Green: Bowling Green State University Popular Press, 1982), 89.

2. C. L. Sonnichsen, *From Hopalong to Hud: Thoughts on Western Fiction* (College Station: Texas A. & M. University Press, 1978), 66. See also the dedication page, Forrestine Cooper Hooker, *The Long, Dim Trail* (New York: Alfred A. Knopf, 1920), and the same author's "Foreword" to her other Western, *When Geronimo Rode* (Garden City: Doubleday, Page, 1924), ix–xii.

3. Annette Kolodny, *The Land Before Her: Fantasy and Experience of the American Frontiers, 1630–1860* (Chapel Hill: University of North Carolina Press, 1984), 225.

4. Francis B. Cogan, *All-American Girl: The Ideal of Real Womanhood in Mid-Nineteenth-Century America* (Athens: University of Georgia Press, 1989), 177.

5. "The Roundup," *Western Story Magazine* (February 18, 1928), 133–134; (November 9, 1929), 136; (March 14, 1931), 130; (October 28, 1939), 6.

6. E.g., *Empty Saddles* (New York: Chelsea House, 1929); *Black Wing's Rider* (New York: Alfred H. King, 1934); and *Stirrup Brother* (New York: Alfred H. King, 1935).

7. Leslie A. Fiedler, *Love and Death in the American Novel,* revised edition (New York: Stein and Day, 1966), 312. Omissions mine.

8. Tales by Cherry Wilson about the child and his foster fathers include "Hushaby's Partner," *Western Story Magazine* (hereinafter referred to as *WSM*) (May 29, 1926): 122–133; "A Mother for Pard," *WSM* (August 28,

1926): 105–115; "Little Pard Meets Apache Bill," *WSM* (November 6, 1926): 116–27; "Shootin'-up Sheriff," *WSM* (June 15, 1929): 45–61; "The Face in the Bunk-House Wall," *WSM* (November 30, 1929): 117–130; "Mild and Woolly," *WSM* (January 30, 1930): 40–52; "Pard's Kidnaper" [sic.], *WSM* (November 7, 1931): 108–125. Wilson also wrote several short stories about the Triangle Z hands that did not include Pard.

9. Wilson, "The Face in the Bunk-House Wall," 117.

10. Richard W. Etulain, "The Historical Development of the Western," in *The Popular Western: Essays Toward a Definition,* ed. Richard Etulain and Michael T. Marsden (Bowling Green: Bowling Green State University Popular Press, 1973), 717/25–726/84.

11. The copyright of *Touchstone* is "by Janet Cicchetti and Lillian Ressler." The dust-jacket blurb of *The City* affirms that "Lillian Janet" is the pseudonym of two writers, Lillian Groom and Janet Cicchetti.

Chapter Eight

1. Francis B. Cogan, *All-American Girl: The Ideal of Real Womanhood in Mid-Nineteenth-Century America* (Athens: University of Georgia Press, 1989), 257.

2. John G. Cawelti, *The Six-Gun Mystique* (Bowling Green: Bowling Green State University Popular Press, 1971), 62.

3. Annette Kolodny, *The Lay of the Land: Metaphor as Experience and History in American Life and Letters* (Chapel Hill: University of North Carolina Press, 1975), 6, 8.

4. E.g., see *The Heart of Night Wind,* 41, and *Flame of the Border,* 20.

5. For example, Katharine Newlin Burt, *This Woman and This Man* (New York: Charles Scribner's Sons, 1934), 1, also her *The Branding Iron,* 4; *Hidden Creek,* 174, and *Snow Blind* (Boston: Houghton Mifflin Co., 1919), 168.

6. Sandra Kay Schackel, "Women in Western Films: The Civilizer, the Saloon Singer, and Their Modern Sister," in *Shooting Stars: Heroes and Heroines of Western Film,* ed. Archie P. McDonald (Bloomington: Indiana University Press, 1987), 200.

7. Will Wright, *Six Guns and Society: A Structural Study of the Western* (Berkeley: University of California Press, 1975), 172.

8. *Ibid,* 192.

9. Schackel, "Women in Western Films," 215. Omissions mine.

10. Jane Tompkins, *West of Everything: The Inner Life of Westerns* (New York: Oxford University Press, 1992), 45.

BIBLIOGRAPHY

Fiction

Aiken, Ednah. *The River.* Indianapolis: Bobbs-Merrill Co., 1914.

Bower, B. M. [Bertha Muzzy Sinclair Cowan]. *Chip of the Flying U.* 1906. Reprint. New York: Grosset & Dunlap, n.d.

———. *The Happy Family.* New York: C. W. Villingham Company, 1910.

———. *The Lonesome Trail.* 1909. Reprint. New York: Grosset & Dunlap, n.d.

———. *Flying U Ranch.* 1912. Reprint. New York: Grosset & Dunlap, n.d.

———. *The Ranch at the Wolverine.* 1914. Reprint. New York: A. L. Burt, n.d.

———. *The Flying U's Last Stand.* 1915. Reprint. New York: Grosset & Dunlap, n.d.

———. *Jean of the Lazy A.* Boston: Little, Brown and Co., 1915.

———. *The Phantom Herd.* 1916. Reprint. New York: Grosset & Dunlap, n.d.

———. *Rodeo.* 1928. Reprint. New York: Triangle Books, 1943.

———. *A Starry Night.* Boston: Little, Brown and Co., 1929.

———. *The Family Failing.* Boston: Little, Brown and Co., 1941.

Brand, Max [Frederick Faust]. *Silvertip's Chase.* 1933. Reprint. New York: Warner Books, 1976.

Broderick, Therese. *The Brand: A Tale of the Flathead Reservation.* Seattle: Alice Harriman Co., 1909.

Burt, Katharine Newlin. *The Branding Iron.* Boston: Houghton Mifflin Co., 1919.

———. *Hidden Creek.* Boston: Houghton Mifflin Co., 1920.

———. *Snow Blind.* Boston: Houghton Mifflin Co., 1921.

————. "Herself." In *O. Henry Memorial Award Prize Stories of 1930*, ed. Blanche Colton Williams. Garden City: Doubleday, Doran and Co., 1930.

————. *A Man's Own Country*. Boston: Houghton Mifflin Co., 1931.

————. *The Tall Ladder*. Boston: Houghton Mifflin Co., 1932.

————. *This Woman and This Man*. New York: Charles Scribner's Sons, 1934.

Foote, Mary Hallock. *The Led-Horse Claim: A Romance of a Mining Camp*. Boston: J. R. Osgood, 1883.

————. *A Touch of Sun and Other Stories*. Boston: Houghton Mifflin Co., 1903.

Gregory, Jackson. *Judith of Blue Lake Ranch*. 1917. Reprint. New York: Grosset & Dunlap, 1920.

————. *Redwood and Gold*. New York: Dodd, Mead and Co., 1929.

Grey, Zane. *Riders of the Purple Sage*. 1912. Reprint. New York: Pocket Books, 1980.

————. *To the Last Man*. 1922. Reprint. New York: Harper & Row, 1950.

Hendryx, James B. *The Yukon Kid*. 1933. Reprint. New York: Triangle Books, 1943.

Henry, Will [Henry Wilson Allen]. *The Bear Paw Horses*. 1973. Reprint. New York: Bantam, 1980.

Hooker, Forrestine Cooper. *The Long, Dim Trail*. New York: Alfred A. Knopf, 1920.

Jackson, Helen Hunt [Saxe Holm]. *Saxe Holm's Stories: First Series*. New York: Charles Scribner's Sons, 1873.

Janet, Lillian [Janet Cicchetti and Lillian Ressler]. *Touchstone*. New York: Rinehart & Co., 1947.

————. *The City Beyond Devil's Gate*. New York: Random House, 1950.

Kelly, Florence Finch. *With Hoops of Steel*. 1900. Reprint. New York: Grosset & Dunlap, n.d.

Lewis, Alfred Henry. *Wolfville*. New York: Frederick A. Stokes Co., 1897.

————. *Sandburrs*. New York: Frederick A. Stokes Co., 1900.

————. *Wolfville Days*. New York: Frederick A. Stokes Co., 1902.

————. *Wolfville Nights*. New York: Frederick A. Stokes Co., 1902.

————. *The Black Lion Inn*. New York: R. H. Russell Co., 1903.

————. *Wolfville Folks*. New York: D. Appleton and Co., 1908.

————. *Faro Nell and her Friends: Wolfville Stories*. New York: G. W. Dillingham Co., 1913.

————. *Wolfville Yarns of Alfred Henry Lewis*, ed. Rolfe Humphries and John Humphries. [Ravenna]: Kent State University Press, 1968.

Lockhart, Caroline. *"Me—Smith."* Philadelphia: J. B. Lippincott Co., 1911.

————. *The Lady Doc.* Philadelphia: J. B. Lippincott Co., 1912.

————. *The Full of the Moon.* Philadelphia: J. B. Lippincott Co., 1914.

————. *The Man from the Bitter Roots.* 1915. Reprint. New York: A. L. Burt Co., 1915.

————. *The Fighting Shepherdess.* Boston: Small, Maynard and Co., 1919.

————. *The Dude Wrangler.* Garden City: Doubleday, Page and Co., 1921.

————. *Old West—and New.* Garden City: Doubleday, Doran and Co., 1933.

Maule, Mary K. *The Little Knight of the X Bar B.* Boston: Lothrop, Lee & Shepard Co., 1910.

McElrath, Frances. *The Rustler: A Tale of Love and War in Wyoming.* New York: Funk & Wagnalls Co., 1902.

Miller, Marcia, and Pronzini, Bill, eds. *She Won the West: An Anthology of Frontier Stories by Women.* New York: William Morrow and Co., 1985.

Nye, Nelson. "Gallows Bait." 1935. Reprinted in Nelson Nye, *Wide Loop.* Edited by Keith Deutsch. Kensington, [NY]: Zebra Books, 1978, 207–256.

Overton, Gwendolen. *The Golden Chain.* New York: Macmillan Co., 1903.

————. *The Heritage of Unrest.* 1901. Reprint. Upper Saddle River [NJ]: Gregg Press, 1969.

Parker, Frances. *Marjie of the Lower Ranch.* Boston: C. M. Clark Publishing Co., 1903.

————. *Hope Hathaway: A Story of Western Ranch Life.* Boston: C. M. Clark Publishing Co., 1904.

————. *Winding Waters: The Story of a Long Trail and Strong Hearts.* Boston: C. M. Clark Publishing Co., 1909.

Roe, Vingie E. "The Story on the Factor's Book." *Munsey's Magazine* 36 (October 1906): 48–51.

————. *The Heart of Night Wind.* 1913. Reprint. New York: Grosset & Dunlap, n.d.

————. "Black Thunder." *Collier's Weekly* 56 (October 30, 1915): 7–8, 22–24.

————. "What Happened at El Rancho Verde." *Collier's Weekly* 56 (December 19, 1915): 7–8, 30–31, 33–34.

————. "In Round Stone Valley." *Collier's Weekly* 60 (February 23, 1918): 18–20, 23–24, 26–27.

————. "Surrender." Part 2. *Sunset* 40 (April 1918): 26–28.

————. "That Girl at Enright's." *Sunset* 41 (July 1918): 27–30.

————. "The Lumberjack." *Everybody's Magazine* 39 (December 1918): 18–23, 82–84.

————. *Tharon of Lost Valley.* 1919. Reprint. New York: Grosset & Dunlap, n.d.

————. "Nameless River." Parts 1–5. *McCall's Magazine* (March 1923–July 1923).

————. *Nameless River.* New York: Duffield and Co., 1923.

————. "Shadows of Granite Ridge: The Desperate Bluff." *Western Story Magazine* 37 (September 29, 1923): 96–107.

————. "Shadows of Granite Ridge: White Ears on Guard." *Western Story Magazine* 37 (October 6, 1923): 100–107.

————. *The Splendid Road.* New York: Duffield and Co., 1925.

————. *Flame of the Border.* Garden City: Doubleday, Doran and Co., 1933.

————. *Sons to Fortune.* Garden City: Doubleday, Doran and Co., 1934.

————. *Black Belle Rides the Uplands.* Garden City: Doubleday, Doran and Co., 1935.

————. *Glory in the Gum Woods.* London: Cassell, 1937.

————. *The Golden Tide.* London: Cassell, 1940.

————. *Wild Harvest.* 1941. Reprint. New York: Grosset & Dunlap, n.d.

————. *Wild Hearts.* Garden City: Doubleday, Doran and Co., 1932.

————. *A Woman of the Great Valley.* London: Cassell, 1956.

Ryan, Marah Ellis. *Squaw Élouise.* Chicago: Rand, McNally & Co., 1892.

————. *The Bondwoman.* 1899. Reprint. Chicago: Rand McNally & Co., 1899.

Willsie, Honoré [Honoré Willsie Morrow]. *The Heart of the Desert.* 1912. Reprint. New York: A. L. Burt Co., 1913.

————. "The Schooling of Isabel Dawes, Spinster." *Delineator* 85 (September 1914): 8, 41.

————. *Still Jim.* 1914. Reprint. New York: A. L. Burt Co., 1915.

————. *The Forbidden Trail.* 1919. Reprint. New York: A. L. Burt Co., 1919.

————. "Desert Justice." *Everybody's Magazine* 45 (September 1921): 99–134.

————. "Breaking the Blue Roan." *Everybody's Magazine* 45 (December 1921): 4–16.

————. "The Adopted Mother." *Century* 104 (September 1922): 654–668.

————. *Judith of the Godless Valley.* New York: Frederick A. Stokes, 1922.

————. *The Exile of the Lariat.* New York: Frederick A. Stokes, 1923.

Wilson, Cherry. "Hushaby's Partner." *Western Story Magazine* 61 (May 29, 1926): 122-133.

————. "A Mother for Pard." *Western Story Magazine* 63 (August 28, 1926): 105–115.

———. "Little Pard Meets Apache Bill." *Western Story Magazine* 64 (November 6, 1926): 116–127.

———. "Shootin'-up Sheriff." *Western Story Magazine* 87 (June 15, 1929): 45–61.

———. "Stormy Dorn." Parts 1–4. *Western Story Magazine* 90 (October 12, 1929): 1–19; (October 19, 1929): 39–59; (October 26, 1929): 40–60; (November 2, 1929): 91–111.

———. "The Face in the Bunk-House Wall." *Western Story Magazine* 91 (November 30, 1929): 117–130.

———. *Empty Saddles*. New York: Chelsea House, 1929.

———. "Mild and Woolly." *Western Story Magazine* 92 (January 30, 1930): 40–52.

———. "Pard's Kidnaper" [sic]. *Western Story Magazine* 103 (November 7, 1931): 108–125.

———. *Black Wing's Rider*. New York: Alfred H. King, Inc., 1934.

———. *Stirrup Brother*. New York: Alfred H. King, Inc., 1935.

Wister, Owen. *Lin McLean*. 1897. Reprint. New York: A. L. Burt, 1907.

———. *The Virginian*. 1902. Reprint. New York: Armed Services Edition, n.d.

Wright, Harold Bell. *The Winning of Barbara Worth*. Chicago: Book Supply Co., 1911.

———. *When a Man's a Man*. Chicago: Book Supply Co., 1916.

Materials Other Than Fiction

Ammons, Elizabeth. *Conflicting Stories: American Women Writers at the Turn Into the Twentieth Century*. New York: Oxford University Press, 1992.

Bakeless, John. *Master of the Wilderness: Daniel Boone*. New York: William Morrow, 1939.

Baym, Nina. "The Women of Cooper's *Leatherstocking* Tales." In *Images of Women in Fiction: Feminist Perspectives*, Edited by Susan Koppleman Cornillon. Bowling Green: Bowling Green State University Popular Press, 1973: 135–154.

———. *Women's Fiction: A Guide to Novels by and About Women in America, 1820–1870*. Ithaca: Cornell University Press, 1978.

———. "Melodramas of Beset Manhood: How Theories of Fiction Exclude Women Authors." *American Quarterly* 33 (1981): 123–139.

Blotner, Joseph. *The Modern American Political Novel 1900–1950*. Austin: University of Texas Press, 1966.

Bold, Christine. *Selling the Wild West: Western fiction 1860 to 1960*. Bloomington: Indiana University Press, 1987.

Bower, B. M. [Bertha Muzzy Sinclair Cowan]. Introduction to *Range Rider*, by Bud Cowan. Garden City: Doubleday, Doran and Co., 1930.

Boyett, Frank. "Courageous or stubborn? Caroline Lockhart wrangles control of 1920s Cody Enterprise, quickly becomes champion of 'Wet' forces." *Cody* [WY] *Enterprise* August 21, 1989: A10.

———. "Lockhart attacks Newton's candidates." *Cody Enterprise* August 23, 1989: B1, B8.

———. "Publisher Lockhart, prosecutor Goppert." *Cody Enterprise* August 28, 1989: B1-B2.

———. "Lockhart, Goppert lock horns again." *Cody Enterprise* August 30, 1989: B1–B2.

Branch, Douglas. *The Cowboy and His Interpreters*. New York: D. Appleton and Co., 1926.

Brown, Herbert Ross. *The Sentimental Novel in America*. Durham: Duke University Press, 1940.

Burt, [Maxwell] Struthers. *The Diary of a Dude Wrangler*. New York: Charles Scribner's Sons, 1924.

Burt, Nathaniel. *Jackson Hole Journal*. Norman: University of Oklahoma Press, 1983.

Carruth, W[illiam]. [Herbert]. *Each in His Own Tongue and Other Poems*. New York: G. P. Putnam's Sons, 1907.

Cawelti, John G. *The Six-Gun Mystique*. Bowling Green: Bowling Green State University Popular Press, 1971.

Chapman, B. B. "A Letter from Vingie E. Roe," Typescript. In Roe "Scrapbook."

Cleaveland, Agnes Morley. *No Life for a Lady*. Boston: Houghton Mifflin Co., 1941.

Cobbs, John L. *Owen Wister*. Twayne United States Authors Series, Vol. 475. Boston: Twayne Publishers, 1983.

Cogan, Frances B. "Weak Fathers and Other Beasts: An Examination of the American Male in Domestic Novels 1850–1870." *American Studies* 25 (1984): 5–20.

———. *All-American Girl: The Ideal of Real Womanhood in Mid-Nineteenth-Century America*. Athens: University of Georgia Press, 1989.

Conant, Roger. *Mercer's Belles: The Journal of a Reporter*, ed. Lenna A. Deutsch. Seattle: University of Washington Press, 1960.

Connelly, Robert B., ed. *Silent Films 1910–1946*. Chicago: Cinébooks, 1986.

Cooper, F. T. Review of *The Heart of Night Wind* by Vingie E. Roe. *Bookman* 37 (May 1913): 339.

Cornillon, Susan Koppelman, ed. *Images of Women in Fiction: Perspectives.* Bowling Green: Bowling Green State University Popular Press, 1973.

David, Saul. "The West of Haycox Westerns." *Roundup* 12 (May 1964): 2, 4–5.

Davison, Stanley R. "The Author Was a Lady." *Montana: The Magazine of Western History* 23 (Spring 1973): 2–15.

"Death Stills Pen of Caroline Lockhart." *Cody Enterprise* (August 2, 1962): 1, 4.

Dimmitt, Richard Bertrand. *A Title Guide to the Talkies: A Comprehensive Listing of 16,000 Feature-Length Films from October 1927, Until December 1963.* Vol. 2. New York: Scarecrow Press, 1965.

Dinan, John A. *The Pulp Western: A Popular History of the Western Magazine in America.* San Bernardino: Borgo Press, 1983.

D. L. M. Review of the *Fighting Shepherdess* by Caroline Lockhart. *Boston Transcript* (March 29, 1919): 9.

Dobie, J. Frank. *Guide to Life and Literature in the Southwest.* Austin: University of Texas Press, 1943.

DuPlessis, Rachel Blau. *Writing Beyond the Ending: Narrative Strategies of Twentieth-Century Women Writers.* Bloomington: Indiana University Press, 1983.

Ernest, Earnest. *The American Eve in Fact and Fiction 1775–1914.* Urbana: University of Illinois Press, 1974.

Eldridge, Paul R. "The Incomparable Vingie." Typescript. In Sonoma County [CA] Library, Cloverdale Regional Branch, Cloverdale, CA.

Elson, Ruth Miller. *Myths and Mores in American Best Sellers 1865–1965.* New York: Garland Publishing Co., 1985.

Engen, Orrin: *Writer of the Plains (A Biography of B. M. Bower).* Culver City: Pontine Press, 1973.

Etulain, Richard W. "A Dedication to . . . Zane Grey 1872–1939." *Arizona and the West* 12 (1970): 217–220. Omission mine.

———. "The Historical Development of the Western." In *The Popular Western: Essays Toward a Definition,* ed. Richard W. Etulain and Michael T. Marsden. Bowling Green: Bowling Green State University Popular Press, 1974.

Falke, Anne. "The Art of Convention: Images of Women in the Modern Western Novels of Henry Wilson Allen." *North Dakota Quarterly* 42 (Spring 1974): 17–27.

Fiedler, Leslie A. *Love and Death in the American Novel.* Revised edition. New York: Stein and Day, 1966.

Gilbert, Sandra M., and Gubar, Susan. *The Madwoman in the Attic: The Woman Writer and the Nineteenth-Century Literary Imagination.* New Haven: Yale University Press, 1979.

Gruber, Frank. *The Pulp Jungle.* Los Angeles: Sherbourne Press, 1967.

Hamblen, Abigail Ann. "Honoré Willsie Morrow." In *American Women Writers,* ed. Barbara White. Vol. 3. New York: Garland, 1977.

Hanson, Patricia King, and Alan Gevinson, eds. *The American Film Institute Catalog of Motion Pictures Produced in the United States: Feature Films 1911–1920.* Berkeley: University of California Press, 1988.

Herr, Pamela. "Reformer." In *The Women Who Made the West: By the Western Writers of America* 1980. Reprint. New York: Avon Discus Books, 1981.

Hicks, Lucille Patrick. *Caroline Lockhart: Liberated Lady—1870–1962.* Cheyenne: Pioneer Printing and Stationery Co., 1984.

Hilfer, Anthony Channell. *The Revolt from the Village 1915–1930.* Chapel Hill: University of North Carolina Press, 1969.

"Honoré Willsie Morrow, Writer on Lincoln." *New York Times* (April 13, 1940): L17.

Jackson, Helen Hunt [Saxe Holm]. *Saxe Holm's Stories: First Series.* New York: Charles Scribner's Sons, 1873.

Johnson, Lee Ann. "Mary Hallock Foote." In *American Women Writers,* ed. Barbara White. Vol. 2. New York: Frederick Ungar, 1980.

Jones, Daryl. *The Dime Novel Western.* Bowling Green: Bowling Green State University Popular Press, 1978.

Jordan, Teresa. *Cowgirls: Women of the American West.* Garden City: Doubleday Anchor Books, 1982.

Kolodny, Annette. *The Lay of the Land: Metaphor as Experience and History in American Life and Letters.* Chapel Hill: University of North Carolina Press, 1975.

———. *The Land Before Her: Fantasy and Experience of the American Frontiers 1630–1860.* Chapel Hill: University of North Carolina Press, 1984.

Kunitz, Stanley J., and Harold Haycraft. *Twentieth Century Authors,* 6th ed. New York: H. W. Wilson, 1966.

Leisy, Ernest E. *The American Historical Novel.* Norman: University of Oklahoma Press, 1960.

Lorimer, George H. *Letters from a Self-Made Merchant to His Son.* Boston: Small, Maynard & Co., 1902.

Margon, Arthur. "Changing Modes of Heroism in Popular American Novels 1880–1920." *American Studies* 17 (Fall 1976): 71–86.

Masteller, Jean Carwile. "The Woman Doctors of Howells, Phelps, and Jewett: The Conflict of Marriage and Career." In *Critical Essays on Sarah Orne Jewett*, ed. Gwen L. Nagel. Boston: G. K. Hall & Co., 1984.

Merton, Robert W. "A Biographical Sketch of Vingie E. Roe." Typescript. In Vingie E. Roe papers, Oklahoma State University library, Stillwater, OK.

Meyer, Roy W. "B. M. Bower: The Poor Man's Wister." In *The Popular Western: Essays Toward a Definition*, ed. Richard W. Etulain and Michael T. Marsden. Bowling Green: Bowling Green State University Popular Press, 1974, 666/24–679/37.

Milton, John R. *The Novel of the American West*. Lincoln: University of Nebraska Press, 1980.

Modleski, Tania. *Feminism Without Women: Culture and Criticism in a "Postfeminist" Age*. New York and London: Routledge, 1991.

"Mrs. Lawton Writes Novels While Husband Sweeps and Makes the Beds." *Medford* [OR] *Mail-Tribune* (February 25, 1912): 7, 11.

Muller, Marcia, and Bill Pronzini, eds. *She Won the West: An Anthology of Western & Frontier Stories by Women*. New York: William Morrow and Co., 1985.

Munden, Kenneth W., ed. *The American Film Institute Catalog of Motion Pictures Produced in the United States: Feature Films 1921–1930*. New York: R. R. Bowker Co., 1971.

Norwood, Vera, and Janice Monk, eds. *The Desert Is No Lady*. New Haven: Yale University Press, 1987.

Nye, Russel B. *The Unembarrassed Muse: The Popular Arts in America*. New York: Dial Press, 1970.

Oliver, Jennie Harris. "Vingie E. Roe." *Daily Oklahoman* (August 16, 1925). In Roe "Scrapbook."

Overton, Grant. "She Pioneered in Novels." *Mentor* 15 (July 1927): 58–59.

Papashvily, Helen Waite. *All the Happy Endings: A Study of the Domestic Novel in America, the Women Who Wrote it, The Women Who Read It in the Nineteenth Century*. 1956. Reprint. New York: Harper & Row, 1971.

Peterson, Joyce Shaw. "Working Girls and Millionaires: The Melodramatic Romances of Laura Jean Libby." *American Studies* 24 (Spring 1983): 19–35.

Phillips, Jr., Raymond C. *Struthers Burt*. Boise State University Western Writers Series 56. Boise: Boise State University Press, 1983.

Phillips, Robert. *Louis L'Amour: His Life and Trails*. 1989. Reprint. New York: Knightsbridge Publishing Company, 1990.

Prairie Gold: By Iowa Authors and Artists. Chicago: Reilly & Britton Co., 1917.

Ravitz, Abe C. *Alfred Henry Lewis*. Boise State University Western Writers Series 32. Boise: Boise State University Press, 1978.

Reep, Diana. *The Rescue and Romance: Popular Novels Before World War I.* Bowling Green: Bowling Green State University Popular Press, 1982.

Review of *The Branding Iron,* by Katharine Newlin Burt. *Nation* 109 (August 23, 1920): 252.

Review of *The Fighting Shepherdess,* by Caroline Lockhart. *New York Times* (May 11, 1919): 271.

Review of *The Fighting Shepherdess,* By Caroline Lockhart. *Springfield Republican* (August 3, 1919): 17.

Review of *The Heart of Night Wind,* by Vingie E. Roe. *New York Sun* (May 17, 1913): 3.

Review of *The Heart of Night Wind,* by Vingie E. Roe. *New York Times* (July 20, 1913): 405.

Review of *Judith of the Godless Valley,* by Honoré Willsie. *Current Opinion* 73 (November 1922): 593.

Review of *The Lady Doc,* by Caroline Lockhart. *New York Times* (October 27, 1912): 628.

Review of *"Me—Smith,"* by Caroline Lockhart, *New York Times* (March 19, 1911): 155.

Review of *"Me—Smith,"* by Caroline Lockhart. *Review of Reviews* 43 (June 1911): 758.

Review of *Nameless River* by Vingie E. Roe. *New York Times* (July 23, 1923): 18.

Review of *Nameless River,* by Vingie E. Roe. *Boston Transcript* (October 10, 1923): 4.

Reynolds, David S. *Beneath the American Renaissance: The Subversive Imagination in the Age of Emerson and Melville.* Cambridge: Harvard University Press, 1989.

Robinson, Lillian S. "Treason Our Text: Feminist Challenges to The Literary Canon." In *The New Feminist Criticism: Essays on Women, Literature, and Theory,* ed. Elaine Showalter. New York: Pantheon Books, 1985, 105–121.

Roe, Vingie E. "Vingie E. Roe: By Herself." *Sunset* (March 1918): 21.

Roe, Vingie E., et al. "Scrapbook." Typescript. Oklahoma State University Library, Stillwater, OK.

"The Roundup" [editorial column]. *Western Story* (February 18, 1928): 133–134; (November 9, 1929): 136; (March 14, 1931): 130; (October 28, 1939): 6.

Russ, Joanna. "What Can a Heroine Do? Or Why Women Can't Write." In Cornillon, *Images,* 3–20.

Schackel, Sandra Kay. "Women in Western Films: The Civilizer, The Saloon Singer, and Their Modern Sister." In *Shooting Stars: Heroes and Heroines of Western Film,* ed. Archie P. McDonald. Bloomington: Indiana University Press 1987, 196–217.

Showalter, Elaine. *A Literature of Their Own: British Women Novelists from Brontë to Lessing.* Princeton: Princeton University Press, 1977.

———. "Women's Time, Women's Space: Writing the History of Feminist Criticism." *Tulsa Studies in Women's Literature* 3 (Spring/Fall 1984): 29–43.

———. "Feminist Criticism in the Wilderness." In *The New Feminist Criticism: Essays on Women, Literature, and Theory,* ed. Elaine Showalter. New York: Pantheon Books, 1985, 243–270.

Shryock, Richard Harrison. *Medicine in America: Historical Essays.* Baltimore: Johns Hopkins University Press, 1966.

Smith, Henry Nash. *Virgin Land: The American West as Symbol and Myth.* 1950. Reprint. New York: Vintage Books, 1957.

Sochen, June. *The New Woman: Feminism in Greenwich Village 1910–1920.* New York: Quadrangle Books, 1972.

Sonnichsen, C. L. *From Hopalong to Hud: Thoughts on Western Fiction.* College Station: Texas A&M University Press, 1978.

Spenser, Edmund. *Complete Poetical Works,* ed. R.E. Neil Dodge. 1908. Reprint. Boston: Houghton Mifflin Co., 1936.

Spiller, Robert E., et al. *Literary History of the United States: Bibliography.* 3rd edition, revised. New York: Macmillan Co., 1974.

Spring, Agnes Wright. "White Woman-Boss." *Sunset* (October 1923): 41.

Tompkins, Jane. "West of Everything." *South Atlantic Quarterly* 86 (Fall 1987): 357–377.

———. *West of Everything: The Inner Life of Westerns.* New York: Oxford University Press, 1992.

"Tragedy of a Godless Childhood." *Literary Digest* 76 (March 31, 1923): 31–32.

Unruh, John D. *The Plains Across: The Overland Emigrants and the Trans-Mississippi West 1840–1890.* Urbana: University of Illinois Press, 1979.

"Vingie E. Roe recalls days at Carney." In Roe, "Scrapbook."

"Vingie E. Roe, 78, Novelist, Dies."*Cloverdale* [CA] *Reveille* (August 14, 1958): 1, 6.

Wasserstrom, William. *Heiress of All the Ages: Sex and Sentiment in the Genteel Tradition.* Minneapolis: University of Minnesota Press, 1959.

Walton, Theodocia. Untitled brief in "Interesting Westerners." *Sunset* (April 1921): 47.

Watt, Roberta Frye. *Four Wagons West: The Story of Seattle.* Portland: Metropolitan Press, 1931.

Welter, Barbara. *Dimity Convictions: The American Woman in the Nineteenth Century.* Athens: Ohio University Press, 1976.

Willsie, Honoré [Honoré Willsie Morrow]. "Women and Food Deterioration." *Collier's Weekly* 49 (April 29, 1912): 22–25.

———. "What Is an American?" Part II. *Collier's* 50 (November 9, 1912): 13–14, 42.

———. "What Is an American?" Part III. *Collier's* 50 (November 16, 1912): 17, 22, 24.

———. "The Women's Vote." *Delineator* 92 (March 1918): 3.

———. "Chapters from Unwritten Autobiographies . . . Book Hunger." *Bookman* 59 (May 1924): 306–310.

———. "God in the Darkness." *Cosmopolitan* 83 (November 1927): 62–63, 164–168.

———. "The Strangest Adventure a Woman Ever Had." *American Magazine* 107 (January 1929): 24–27, 80, 82, 84, 86.

———. "I Learned About God from a Negress." *Cosmopolitan* 86 (March 1929): 28–29, 144, 146, 148–150.

Wister, Owen. *Lin McLean.* 1897. Reprint. New York: A. L. Burt Co., 1907.

———. *Members of the Family.* 1911. Reprint. New York: Macmillan, 1923.

———. "To Sarah Butler Wister." July 5, 1902. Unnumbered letter in *Owen Wister Out West,* ed. Fanny Kemble Wister. Chicago: University of Chicago Press, 1958.

Wright, Harold Bell. *The Winning of Barbara Worth.* Chicago: Book Supply Co., 1911.

———. *When a Man's a Man.* Chicago: Book Supply Co., 1916.

Wright, Kathryn. "Author Caroline Lockhart Dies in Cody at 91 Years." *Billings* [MT] *Gazette* (December 26, 1962): 2, 5.

Wright, Will. *Six Guns and Society: A Structural Study of the Western.* Berkeley: University of California Press, 1975.

INDEX